Reclaiming Your REAL Identity

When Trauma Steals What's Rightfully Yours

BETHANY ELLE

ISBN: 979-8-9919424-7-8
eBook: 979-8-9919424-6-1

Dedication

To my husband, who stood beside me with unwavering love as I reclaimed everything the enemy tried to steal. Your strength gave me courage, and your faith held me steady.

To Bunnie, the mom of my heart.

To my dear friends, Colleen and Laura, thank you for your prayers, presence, and belief in the woman I was becoming.

And to every reader, may these pages lead you closer to the identity God intended for you. You are not forgotten. You are not too far gone. You are called, chosen, and deeply loved.

About the Author

Bethany Elle is a best-selling author, national speaker, and certified identity trauma coach. She is also the founder and director of Agape Celebration, a non-profit ministry for women.

She is the mother of five, grandmother of six, and has been married to her college sweetheart for over 40 years.

Bethany's mission is REAL:

Rooted.**E**mpowered.**A**uthentic.**L**oved.

She chooses to be a light to all those around her, to live a life of hope through adversity, help others understand their identity, and to leave a legacy for her family and friends.

Contents

Introduction

There are mornings when you wake up and the person in the mirror feels unfamiliar. You open the closet and stare at your clothes, no longer sure what you like or what fits who you are. The things you once loved—music, food, laughter—feel distant, almost as if they belonged to someone else. You stand in the middle of your life and wonder, "Where did I go?" If you know this feeling, you are not alone.

Trauma changes many things. It can sweep in quietly or crash down suddenly, leaving you feeling lost, empty, or disconnected from yourself. You might doubt your own feelings or struggle to trust your judgment. Maybe you notice shame or self-blame that lingers, or you find yourself pulling away from people, isolating in hopes of feeling safe. Boundaries blurred. Joy fades. The world feels unpredictable, and your sense of self slips further away.

I wrote this book because I have spent years walking alongside people who carry these invisible burdens. Through my work supporting adults—women and men—recovering from trauma, I have seen firsthand how deep the struggle with identity loss can go. Again and again, I have heard the same questions: "Who am I now?" and "Will I ever feel whole again?" I am passionate about helping you find answers that are real, practical, and rooted in understanding. You deserve more than vague advice or empty promises. You deserve tools that honor your story and real hope that healing is possible.

This book is for you if you have ever felt like a stranger in your own life. It is for anyone who feels empty inside, doubts their feelings, or wrestles with shame that will not lift. It is for those who withdraw from friends and family, who struggle to set boundaries, or who live with a constant hum of anxiety. If you have tried to "move on" or forced yourself to forget the past, only to feel worse, you are not alone. If you fear that exploring your story will make things worse, or you find it hard to connect with others, you belong here.

You may have tried many solutions already. Maybe you have read self-help books that offer quick fixes or joined programs that promise transformation in thirty days. Perhaps you have tried ignoring the pain, hoping it would fade on its own, or pulled away from others to protect yourself. These paths can bring comfort for a moment, but they often fall short for those healing from trauma. Trauma recovery is not about quick fixes or one-size-fits-all plans. It is about patient, steady steps toward reclaiming what is rightfully yours—your true identity.

This book offers a different way forward. You will find step-by-step tools you can use daily, not just in theory. You will meet real people who have walked this path before you. Their stories and case studies are as diverse as the readers who will pick up these pages. You will discover reflection prompts, journaling exercises, and micro-steps that let you move at your own pace. The structure is flexible, so you can return to chapters as needed. This is not a rigid program. It is a guide that meets you where you are.

Setbacks are part of any healing journey. You may move forward and then feel like you have slipped back. This is not a failure. Every attempt to reconnect with yourself is a sign of courage. Healing is not a straight line. It bends, twists, and sometimes circles back. Each step is worth taking, even when it feels small.

You will find the book organized into clear, practical chapters. We start by understanding how trauma steals your sense of self. Then we look at ways to gently reconnect with your mind and body. I will share tools for self-compassion and acceptance, and we will explore how to build and protect healthy boundaries. You will learn ways to connect authentically with others and find hope for the future. There is space for spiritual reflection, including the role of prayer and scripture, for those who seek it. Each chapter ends with simple steps you can try right away.

I invite you to use this book as a companion on your journey. Try the exercises. Pause for the journal prompts. Take the micro-steps, even if they seem small at first. There is no right or wrong way to move through these pages. Some days, you may want to read, and others, you may simply reflect. Bring your questions, doubts, and hopes.

Reclaiming your real identity after trauma is not easy. Some days will be hard, and some days, you will feel progress. Both are signs that you are moving forward. You are not broken. You are not alone. With patience and support, real transformation and joy are possible. My hope is that these pages will walk with you, offering guidance, validation, and practical help every step of the way.

You have already shown courage by picking up this book. Let's begin together.

As a Christian life coach and author, my journey has been profoundly shaped by God's love and the truth in His Word. Throughout this book, you'll discover a variety of practical tools and restorative practices—each one, I believe, becomes even more transformative when rooted in a relationship with God. I sincerely hope that, as you work through these pages, you will experience not only practical healing, but also the deep comfort and hope that God's love brings. My prayer is that you feel the gentle presence of God alongside you as you reclaim your real identity.

Read on to discover the meaning of REAL

1. Understanding the Shattered Self

You may recall a morning when simply choosing between cream or sugar for your coffee felt strangely difficult, or flipping through your playlist without any song sparking joy, or nodding along in a conversation but feeling detached, as if watching someone else's life. These aren't just signs of a bad mood—they point to identity disruption. Identity is the invisible thread connecting your preferences, values, quirks, and dreams into a sense of "me." Trauma doesn't just rattle your emotions; it fractures this thread, scattering your sense of self into disconnected fragments.

What Trauma Steals: Identity Disruption Demystified

For many, trauma isn't just a single event. It quietly invades your daily life and alters everything you think you know about yourself. Imagine your identity as a mirror reflecting your personality, interests, strengths, and flaws. Before trauma, that mirror may have been clear; you recognized yourself—your favorite foods, humor, and stress responses. Trauma is like a crack in glass. Sometimes it shatters all at once from loss, assault, or disaster. Other times it fractures slowly, each painful event adding another break. Eventually, your reflection becomes warped or even unrecognizable.

Identity disruption isn't just about sadness or anxiety. You may forget what used to bring you joy or lose touch with passions like painting, hiking, or reading, as though they're no longer accessible.

Your values blur; you second-guess what matters or wonder if your priorities ever really belonged to you. Even minor choices—what to eat, what to watch—might feel like unanswerable questions.

It's common to blame yourself for this confusion, but it's important to understand identity disruption after trauma is not weakness or a character flaw—it's a survival response. When pain or threat becomes overwhelming, your mind and body protect you by shutting down memories or numbing preferences that once were safe but now feel dangerous. Experts call this "protective amnesia"—an adaptive form of forgetting, which shields you from distress when life is too much (see [22] in APA list). This isn't laziness or failure—it's biology doing its best.

Identity loss after trauma is far more common than most people realize. I've heard stories from people of all ages and backgrounds: a young woman who wondered, "I used to know what I stood for—now I'm not sure I stand for anything," a retired woman who questioned, "Was I always this quiet before everything happened?" and a friend, after memories of childhood abuse, admitted, "Sometimes I feel like I'm just playing a role in my own home." These aren't rare experiences. Survivors of all genders, cultures, and trauma types share them.

The shift can be sudden—you "wake up" from surviving for years and feel disconnected from your job, partner, or home. Or it can erode you slowly, enduring a toxic relationship or stressful job until your uniqueness is worn away by criticism or fear. Outsiders often don't notice, because this process is mostly invisible. You might still go to work, joke at dinner, or post on social media, all while feeling empty inside.

What's happening is an adaptation. Your sense of self shifts to protect you from further pain or threat. Key parts of your identity retreat, shielding yourself from reminders of past hurts, even if that means losing pieces of what made you, you. This is why memories disappear and old hobbies lose their appeal. Your brain and body work together to steer clear of pain, sometimes at the cost of your personality.

Reflection Exercise: Noticing What's Missing

Take a moment to write down three things you used to enjoy or care about before your trauma—big or small. Maybe it was a favorite movie genre, gardening, or how you liked to spend weekends. Next to each, note how connected (or disconnected) you feel to them today. Notice any emotions or patterns.

You don't need all the answers. The point is to notice what has changed—and know that these changes are not your fault.

Identity disruption after trauma is both universal and uniquely personal. Some feel it instantly, like an earthquake; others think it sneaks in over the years. However it looks for you, these feelings are valid. There's nothing wrong with needing help to find your missing pieces again.

Why You Feel "Empty"—The Neuroscience of Numbness

There's a moment you might recognize, maybe it comes when you stare at a meal and realize you're not hungry, though you haven't eaten all day. Or you sit in front of the TV, flipping through channels, feeling nothing at all. Even the hobbies that once brought comfort now seem pointless, like faded photographs tucked in a drawer. This hollow, flat sensation isn't laziness or giving up. It's not a lack of willpower or caring. It's your brain working overtime to protect you from pain that once felt impossible to bear.

Here's what happens beneath the surface: trauma overloads the brain's alarm system, which lives in a deep region called the amygdala. That alarm sends signals throughout your entire nervous system, telling you, "Danger—prepare for threat." In the thick of trauma, this warning is lifesaving. But when the threat isn't just a single moment—when it drags on, repeats, or never feels fully resolved—the brain can't stay in high alert forever. It responds by flipping a kind of internal circuit breaker. This "breaker" cuts off the signals before they reach your emotional center, producing numbness. The psychological term is hypoarousal—a state where emotions, memories, and even body sensations get dialed down or switched off.

Another word for this response is dissociation. You might notice yourself spacing out, forgetting chunks of time, or feeling detached from your thoughts and feelings as if watching life from behind a foggy window. Some people describe it as "going blank" during arguments or stressful moments. Others notice their bodies moving through the motions—showering, working, caring for kids—but inside, it feels like nothing matters. This is not you failing at life; it's biology's way of keeping the emotional overload from frying your circuits.

Understanding why this happens helps to know about the "window of tolerance." Imagine this window as your natural range for handling life's ups and downs. Inside the window, you can feel stress, sadness, or excitement and still function. Trauma narrows that window drastically. Stress or reminders push you out of it—sometimes into panic or rage (hyperarousal), but just as often into numbness and shutdown (hypoarousal). The brain shuts out overwhelming feelings to protect you from reliving old pain.

Short-term, this numbing has a purpose: it helps you survive what felt unsurvivable. It's a shield that blocks pain, fear, or grief from flooding your system when you have no power to escape or fight back. Long-term, though, it becomes its own kind of prison. Emotional numbness doesn't just block sadness or terror—it also blocks joy, curiosity, and love. It's like living in a house where every light switch has been flipped off to prevent a fire, but now you're left in the dark.

If you wonder why you can't feel excitement about anything or why even good news brings only a faint echo of happiness, this is the reason. The brain doesn't filter emotions with precision; when the circuit breaker flips, everything gets muted. Over time, this constant dullness erodes your sense of self. If you can't feel your own reactions—if hunger, anger, pride, or hope all blend into gray—how do you know what you want? How can you set boundaries if your gut never sends clear signals? This is the hidden link between emotional numbness and loss of identity: without feelings to guide you, even simple decisions become a guessing game.

It's common to feel frustrated with yourself for this emptiness. You might berate yourself for not caring more about your job or relationships. You may tell yourself to just "snap out of it," but nothing shifts. This frustration is valid and deeply human; it reflects a longing for connection—with yourself and with life again. The truth is that numbness is not a character flaw or permanent state. It is a temporary adaptation that your nervous system learned to keep you safe.

Self-Check: Recognizing Your Signs of Numbness

Take a few minutes to reflect on these questions. Mark any that sound familiar:

- I often eat without tasting my food—or forget meals altogether.
- Hobbies I used to enjoy now feel pointless or exhausting.
- I go through daily routines on autopilot, barely noticing what I'm doing.
- Compliments and good news barely register; I shrug them off.
- I have trouble naming what I'm feeling at any given moment.
- I avoid making decisions because nothing sounds appealing or right.
- Friends' invitations rarely excite me—I mostly say yes or no out of habit.
- I sometimes lose track of time or forget parts of my day.
- Physical pain or pleasure feels muted or distant.
- Self-care tasks (bathing, changing clothes, brushing teeth) seem unnecessary.

If several of these ring true, know that you're not alone—this pattern is widespread among trauma survivors. It reflects a nervous system doing its best to keep you functional when everything feels overwhelming.

Understanding this connection between neurobiology and numbness is one step toward compassion—for yourself and for your body's efforts to protect you. This isn't brokenness; it's evidence that your mind cares deeply about your survival. With time and gentle support, it's possible to widen that "window" and invite life's colors back in—even if only one shade at a time.

The Hidden Impact: How Trauma Warps Self-Perception

One of the most persistent and sneaky effects of trauma is how it twists the way you see yourself. This isn't about facts or logic—it's about the private, relentless story that runs through your mind. For many, that story is not kind. Long after the actual threat has faded, an inner voice lingers, whispering judgments and doubts. It tells you, "You should have known better," or "This happened because you let it." Sometimes this voice is harsh and loud, other times it's subtle, almost reasonable, but it always carries a weight of blame. You start to believe that your pain is a result of your own mistakes or shortcomings. Shame settles in, heavy and stubborn. Self-blame becomes a reflex, firing up even when logic says you weren't at fault.

Trauma plants seeds that grow into distorted beliefs about worth and lovability. These beliefs sneak into everyday situations—catching you off-guard when you least expect it. Maybe you start to think you're "too much" for people to handle, or that you're "not enough" to keep someone around. Sometimes you walk on eggshells, convinced that other people's moods are your responsibility. If someone seems annoyed or distant, your mind jumps to the conclusion that you did something wrong. An old friend described the feeling as "constantly scanning faces for signs I've failed." This isn't vanity or hypersensitivity—it's a learned survival skill. When someone has lived through betrayal, criticism, or emotional neglect, their radar becomes finely tuned for disappointment or rejection. You might find yourself shrinking back after sharing an idea at work if your boss merely nods instead of smiling. A neutral response feels like failure. Even small misunderstandings with friends can spiral into hours of self-criticism.

These patterns don't appear overnight. They take root when trauma teaches you that safety depends on avoiding mistakes, reading others' signals, and never letting your guard down. Over time, this vigilance seeps into how you interpret every interaction. Trusting your own judgment becomes risky. You start to question not just what you feel, but whether what you feel is even valid. "Did I really hear them correctly? Am I overreacting?" This second-guessing doesn't just make life more stressful—it makes it harder to know what you need or want in the first place.

Take the example of someone who grew up feeling responsible for a parent's happiness. Later in life, they might apologize even when they haven't done anything wrong, or they might take on blame at work just to keep the peace in the office. Another survivor described how even praise felt suspicious: "If someone complimented me, I'd immediately wonder what they wanted from me—or assume they were just being polite." It's exhausting to live this way, always doubting your own instincts.

The "inner critic" is one of trauma's most loyal companions. For some, it sounds like a parent or authority figure from the past. For others, it's an echo of every time trust was broken or boundaries were ignored. This critic doesn't just point out mistakes—it rewrites your entire life story to make you the villain or the weak link. If something goes wrong in a relationship, it must be proof that you're unlovable. If a project at work falls apart, it's evidence that you'll never succeed.

These "false stories" burrow deep and become hard to challenge because they feel so familiar.

Hypervigilance—being constantly on alert—might have helped keep you safe once. Now it makes you question every gut feeling, every preference, every decision. You may replay conversations in your head, searching for clues that you missed something important or did something wrong. This isn't overthinking for its own sake; it's a way to predict pain before it arrives. But it comes at a cost: your confidence takes hit after hit, and trusting yourself starts to feel impossible.

Many survivors describe this as feeling like a stranger in their own lives. Imagine waking up one day and realizing that the person making choices, speaking up (or staying silent), even dressing themselves, isn't entirely "you." Your reflection in the mirror looks familiar but foreign at the same time. A woman once shared how she couldn't recognize her own laugh in a group meeting—it felt staged, as if she was watching someone else enjoy life while she observed from the sidelines.

It's important to know that these shifts in self-perception are common after trauma and not a personal failure. If you feel lost, if you doubt your worth or question whether anyone could love the "real" you, please know these are symptoms—not facts about who you are.

Reflection Prompt:

Think back to a recent situation where you hesitated before making a choice or doubted your first instinct—no matter how small. Write out what happened and what your inner critic said in that moment. Then ask yourself: "If I could silence that voice for just one minute, what would I want—or believe—about myself instead?" Notice if new words or feelings come up when the critic steps aside, even briefly.

You don't have to fix everything right now. Naming these patterns is a powerful step toward reclaiming the way you see yourself—warts and all—and realizing those false stories do not have to be the end of your narrative.

Over-Identifying with the Victim: When Survival Becomes Identity

After trauma, an invisible heaviness can settle in, much like wearing a thick winter coat long after the cold has passed. That coat was once essential for safety, but as life changes, it can start to feel fused to your skin, weighing you down even when you want to move freely. This is what it's like when the identity of "survivor" or "victim" shifts from being an experience to the main lens through which you see yourself and your world.

At first, adopting a victim or survivor's identity makes sense. It can explain why things are hard, provide reason to grieve, and allow you to accept compassion. This role initially acts as a shield; being able to identify as someone who was hurt serves a purpose, creating space for rest, understanding, and perhaps even belonging.

However, a subtle problem arises when survival becomes your entire story. The very coat that kept you safe now limits your movement and blurs your true shape. You might hold back from making plans or pursuing dreams, finding it safer to expect disappointment than to risk hope. Setting goals or imagining a brighter future feels threatening if you've been let down before. Keeping expectations low and retreating into what's familiar can seem easier than taking chances and risking new pain.

Some people hold onto the victim's identity not out of desire for pity, but because letting go feels like standing unprotected in a storm—far more vulnerable than clinging to pain. If hardship has been constant, even joy or kindness might feel suspicious, as if happiness is merely a bait for future heartbreak.

Living mostly through this single lens is exhausting. It narrows your perspective so much that it eclipses other parts of who you are—like your humor, curiosity, ambition, or tenderness. Many describe feeling unable to imagine any future where trauma is not the main storyline. Picture yourself five years from now without referencing what hurt you—if that feels impossible, the victim identity may have taken center stage. Invitations, relationships, and new experiences are sometimes rejected not out of disinterest, but because the possibility of disappointment outweighs the potential for happiness. The victim role can block hope before it even has a chance to grow.

In relationships, this over-identification can manifest as keeping distance, sabotaging connections, or reacting to support with suspicion: "What do they want from me? Will they leave once they see my true self?" Even moments of happiness can trigger anxiety, making joy itself feel fleeting or dangerous.

Yet recognizing the victim identity as only one part of your whole self is the first step toward change. A helpful concept here is "parts work" from Internal Family Systems (IFS) therapy [see 21 in APA list]. You don't need formal training to use this tool—just imagine your inner world as a team of different voices. The victim part appeared for good reasons: to help you survive and make sense of pain. But other parts—those connected to laughter, adventure, or dreams—are still within you, even if they feel faint or hidden.

Your core self, who you were before the pain, isn't lost; it's simply buried under the layers of protection. The goal isn't to eliminate the victim part—it served its purpose—but to allow other parts back into the picture and reclaim space.

If you feel trapped in survival mode, try a simple exercise: recall a time before the hardship when you felt alive, curious, or whole, no matter how small the moment. Maybe it was a childhood hobby, a song that lifted your spirit, or a core value from long ago. Write down one quality, dream, or value that predates your trauma. Keep it visible—as a note on your mirror, a reminder on your phone, or a slip of paper in your wallet. This exercise isn't about erasing your story but about reminding yourself that your identity holds more than suffering.

Progress will vary—some days you'll move forward, others you may circle back. This is a natural part of rediscovery. With patience and kindness toward yourself, you can begin to shed that heavy coat when it's safe, trusting that resilience and warmth are within you and outside old defenses.

Remember this: Every step forward, no matter how small, is an act of bravery. You are much more than your wounds, and it is possible to let other parts of yourself emerge, giving them space and sunlight to grow.

*In my book, *__When the Church Thinks You're Crazy__*, I share my own experience of feeling detached and empty after trauma—like a* *part of me was missing that nothing seemed able to restore. It wasn't until I surrendered my pain and uncertainty to God, allowing myself to be embraced by His love and reassured by the truths found in Scripture, that I started to heal my fractured sense of self. Trauma had left me locked in a constant state of fear. But as I began intentionally choosing peace over fear—moment by moment—I discovered a new path forward. This journey gradually led me back to the core of my true identity, reclaiming what trauma had stolen.*

There were many days when I poured my heart out in prayer and filled pages with my thoughts, wrestling with a sense of emptiness and wondering if I was even real. It was during one of these quiet moments that a scripture spoke deeply to me: "These are a shadow of the things that were to come; the reality, however, is found in Christ." Colossians 2:17.

As I continued to reflect and seek guidance, I began to ask God what it truly means to be real—to reclaim the wholeness that trauma had stolen. Over time, I sensed an answer forming: REAL stood for Rooted, Empowered, Authentic, Loved. I discovered that when I ground myself in Christ—secure and rooted in the unchanging truths of who He says I am—I began to reconnect with my authentic self, the person I was meant to be. From that place of authenticity, I felt empowered by God's strength to both receive love and extend it to others. This journey toward being REAL is an ongoing process, but each step brings me closer to the person I was always meant to become

2. Naming the Pain

Validating Your Lived Experience

"Am I Alone in This?"—Stories from Diverse Survivors

There's a moment, sometimes late at night, when everything feels silent except your thoughts. You scroll through your phone, maybe glance at photos from years ago, and wonder if anyone else has ever felt the way you do now—untethered, out of place, as if you landed in the middle of someone else's story. The truth is, countless others have asked themselves the same question: "Is it just me?" But pain and confusion after trauma show up in so many forms that it's easy to believe you're the only one struggling.

Consider Jason, a father of two who survived a car accident. Before the crash, he was the go-to guy for friends and family, always quick with a joke or a helping hand. Afterward, he couldn't shake this sense that something essential had gone missing. He said, "I kept thinking I was the only one who felt like a background character in my own life." His laughter faded; his confidence in everyday choices crumbled. He wondered if he'd ever get back to the man he remembered.

Then there's Priya, a young woman who moved countries to go to school. The stress of immigration—learning new customs, missing family, fearing she'd never quite fit in—took a toll on her sense of self. She described feeling invisible in crowded rooms and misunderstood by relatives back home. Priya said, "Everyone thought I was living the dream, but I felt like I was losing pieces of myself every day." Her story isn't about a single catastrophic event but about the slow erosion of identity and belonging.

Luna's trauma began with betrayal by a close friend she'd known since childhood. The loss stung so sharply that she started questioning her own judgment and worth. She shared, "I began replaying every conversation we'd ever had, searching for what I did wrong." Trust became hard currency; she withdrew from new connections, worried she'd never be able to let anyone in again.

For Jasmine, trauma arrived through chronic illness in her twenties. She'd always been athletic and independent until her diagnosis forced her to rely on others for basic tasks. "It wasn't just the pain," she explained. "If I couldn't run or work, I felt unsure who I was. Some days I felt like my body had betrayed me; other days I didn't recognize myself at all." Chronic illness is rarely named in conversations about trauma and identity loss, but it carves deep wounds that don't always show on the surface.

Brian, a middle-aged gay man from a conservative rural community, spent years hiding parts of himself to avoid rejection. When he finally came out, the relief was mixed with grief for all the years spent pretending. "I got so used to shaping myself to what others wanted that I forgot how to be real," Ethan admitted. His struggle wasn't just about sexuality or acceptance; it was about reclaiming authenticity after decades of self-erasure.

Even within one family, experiences can diverge wildly. Take Belle and her brother Daniel, who grew up in a household marked by emotional volatility. Belle responded by becoming the peacemaker—

always pleasant, never demanding anything for herself—while Daniel grew distant, seeking solitude rather than risk conflict. Years later, both described feeling "different" from friends but for opposite reasons: Belle seemed too eager to please; Daniel felt numb and disconnected. Their paths were shaped by the same environment but led to different forms of identity confusion.

Some stories have not one traumatic event but a thousand small moments that chip away at certainty. Rose remembers growing up in a faith community where questioning beliefs wasn't allowed. When she began to doubt, she felt adrift—not only spiritually but personally. "I thought there was something wrong with me for asking questions," she recalls. Her struggle wasn't only about faith but about feeling fundamentally out of step with those around her.

There are survivors whose trauma stemmed from medical emergencies—a sudden surgery gone wrong—or from relentless workplace bullying that left them doubting their own abilities. A retired nurse named Helen described it this way: "After years of being strong for everyone else, I finally broke down when I retired. It hit me that I didn't know who I was outside my job."

Across all these stories, common threads emerge: feeling misunderstood or isolated, losing trust in one's own feelings or decisions, and quietly believing that no one else could possibly relate. Yet unique details color each voice—a different age, culture, or source of pain—but the heartache of wondering "Who am I now?" is universal.

Reflection Invitation

Which story here feels closest to your own? Which feels

furthest—and what do you notice as you read? Take a moment to jot down your reactions or feelings that surface when you see yourself reflected (or not reflected) in these accounts. Notice what resonates and what stands apart; both are important clues in understanding your experience.

No matter where your story began or how it's unfolded, there is nothing wrong with needing validation and connection. Trauma shapes identity in countless ways—none more real or deserving of compassion than another. Each story counts, including yours.

As a mother of five adult children, my deepest desire has always been for their well-being. When one of my sons entered a marriage with a woman struggling with severe mental health challenges, it brought a unique kind of trauma into our family. Witnessing the ongoing abuse—both emotional and physical—while feeling powerless to help in meaningful ways left me feeling lost and deeply unsettled. Over time, I watched my son's sense of self erode under the weight of manipulation, gaslighting, and the constant demands of someone perpetually cast in the role of the victim. Ultimately, his path to healing and reclaiming his true identity began only when he made the difficult choice to walk away and embark on his own journey of recovery. His story is a reminder that reclaiming your real self sometimes requires courageous decisions and the willingness to step into the unknown for the sake of your own well-being.

Naming Invisible Wounds: Recognizing Subtle Traumas

When most people think of "trauma," they picture the obvious—accidents, disasters, acts of violence. These "big-T" traumas are events so significant that they clearly divide life into before and after, leaving no doubt they "count." But trauma also includes quieter hurts that often go unnoticed: "little-t" traumas. These are the subtle, persistent experiences that chip away at your self-worth—chronic criticism, feeling invisible in your own family, or enduring constant microaggressions.

"Little-t" trauma shows up in simple but wounding ways. Maybe your parents provided for you, but were never emotionally available. Perhaps you faced constant teasing at school or subtle exclusion among friends or colleagues. You could have belonged to a faith community where questions were punished, or dealt with continual slights at work that left you doubting your value.

Unlike obvious trauma, these wounds often build slowly and quietly, creating a background hum of anxiety or self-doubt that's easy to ignore until you finally realize how long it's lingered. For many, these subtle hurts damage identity as much as dramatic events do. Yet, because society doesn't label them "trauma," you might dismiss your own struggles, thinking you're overreacting or being weak. Many people compare their "smaller" pain to others' big tragedies and convince themselves they should brush it off.

Neglect is among the most invisible wounds. If there was no yelling or hitting but emotional absence—parents too overwhelmed to notice your feelings—it still leaves a deep mark. Trauma isn't always about what happened; sometimes it's about what never did, like never being soothed when sad or told your feelings mattered. This absence can make you believe your needs are burdensome or that having emotions is wrong.

Chronic invalidation works similarly. If every upset was met with, "don't be so sensitive," or "just get over it," you learn to mute yourself. Hiding pain (and even joy) becomes second nature because seeking attention feels risky or futile.

Bullying, whether overt in childhood or subtle in adulthood, a coworker's sly undermining, being left out by friends, may seem minor to outsiders. But these moments accumulate, making you question your worth or whether reaching out is worthwhile. Microaggressions—those small, dismissive comments about your background or appearance—don't shatter your confidence immediately, but over time, they collectively erode your sense of belonging.

Spiritual abuse is less talked about, but it can deeply affect your relationship with yourself and others. Being taught that parts of you are sinful or unworthy, or being shamed by leaders, leaves a hidden but persistent wound, changing how you see yourself and how hopeful you feel in the world. Spiritual abuse can profoundly distort your understanding of God and erode your sense of self. When your image of a loving Creator is damaged, it can undermine the foundational belief that you are valued and cherished. In these moments, both faith and identity may feel uncertain or uprooted. Healing begins with gently exploring who God truly is, separate from harmful experiences, so you can rediscover your inherent worth and rebuild a sense of trust—in both the Divine and yourself.

A woman I met—let's call her Rachel—spent years assuming she hadn't experienced real trauma. Her parents didn't hit or shout; her needs were met. But she was never told she was loved, her achievements were overlooked, and she always felt like an afterthought. As an adult, Rachel felt disconnected and struggled with relationships. It wasn't until she understood that neglect—the absence of emotional support and validation—could be as harmful as anything overtly traumatic that she started to heal.

We often minimize our pain, thinking, "It wasn't that bad" or "Others have it worse." Sometimes this is because others fail to recognize our wounds; other times, it's a way of protecting ourselves from feeling needy. Suppressing your story, though, only keeps it alive beneath the surface. Honoring both what happened and what didn't occur is an act of self-respect. Your pain doesn't need to be dramatic to deserve attention.

Invisible Wounds Inventory

Take a few quiet moments to reflect and write down anything that surfaces:

- Times you felt unseen or ignored by someone important.
- Moments your feelings were met with "stop overreacting."
- Instances where you hid parts of yourself to feel safe or accepted.
- Days you felt too much—or not enough—for loved ones.
- Situations where "small" jokes or comments chipped at your confidence.
- Memories of longing for comfort and getting silence.
- Achievements that were brushed aside or minimized.

You don't have to finish or recall everything now—the point is to give language to what your heart already feels. These invisible wounds matter. If you find yourself doubting whether your pain "counts," notice where that voice comes from, and consider how healing might begin if you simply allowed your pain to be witnessed instead of being swept away.

You're Not "Too Broken"—Debunking the Myth of Unfixability

There's a belief that creeps in when you've been hurt too many times or when the world has felt unsafe for too long—a whisper that says you're "too broken" to ever really feel whole again. Maybe you've felt it in your bones, that heavy certainty that other people can heal but you, for some reason, are beyond repair. This myth of unfixability is powerful and persistent. It can keep you stuck, make you doubt every small step forward, and sap your hope before you even begin. But here's what's true: being hurt does not make you unworthy of change or incapable of growth. No matter how long you've struggled, your brain and your sense of self are more adaptable than you realize.

Let's look at what science says. Decades of research on neuroplasticity—basically, the brain's ability to change and adapt—have proven that our minds keep learning and rewiring throughout life (see [26] in APA list). Even brains shaped by years of trauma can forge new neural pathways. The old idea that "you can't teach an old dog new tricks" just doesn't hold up anymore. Therapists who work with trauma survivors see this every day, watching people reclaim parts of themselves they thought were lost forever. It takes time, patience, and honesty, but it happens. Sometimes slowly. Sometimes, with setbacks that make progress hard to see until you look back and realize how far you've come.

Jackie spent years believing she was stuck with her numbness and anger. She lost her marriage, fought with friends, and eventually stopped reaching out to anyone at all. When she joined therapy, she said flat out, "I don't think I'm fixable." For months, nothing seemed to change. Small talk felt pointless. She hated every exercise suggested. But somewhere around the six-month mark, something shifted. She found herself laughing—really laughing—at a joke on TV and felt startled by it. It was nothing big on the surface, but for her, these were glimmers of life coming back. Jackie still had rough days. Sometimes she'd slip right back into old patterns and feel discouraged all over again. But those little sparks kept showing up, proof that healing was happening in the background, slow but steady.

Then there's Martha. She carried childhood wounds for decades, believing she was beyond help because her pain had been ignored for so long. She started with online support groups, not ready to trust anyone face-to-face. She'd read stories about growth but never saw herself in them. Still, she kept showing up—even when it felt pointless—and over time she noticed she could ask for what she needed without apologizing. The first time she said "no" to a friend's demand, she expected backlash or abandonment. Instead, her friend respected her boundary—and Martha felt a surge of self-respect she hadn't experienced since childhood.

Healing doesn't look like a straight staircase to freedom or a quick sprint out of darkness; it's more like a spiral—sometimes looping back before moving forward again. There will be days when you feel like you lost ground or even fell apart entirely. But those days are not proof that you're broken beyond repair—they're actually signs that your system is working to process and integrate things at a deeper level.

The Healing Spiral

(Visual: Imagine a spiral moving upward—a line circles back on itself but rises with each loop.)

Setbacks aren't just inevitable; they're part of authentic healing. In fact, many trauma-informed therapists talk about setbacks as moments of hidden progress rather than failure. Here's a quote from one such therapist:
"Every time you revisit an old wound or pattern and respond just a little differently—even if it doesn't feel like much—you're actually rewiring your brain for hope. Healing isn't about never falling down; it's about learning to stand up again and again."
(Sidebar: Setbacks are not proof of failure but markers of growth—your nervous system is trying new ways to cope, even if it feels messy.)

You might notice that when you try something new—speaking up for yourself, reaching out for help—your old patterns scream louder at first. It feels uncomfortable because change always does at the beginning. But over time, those uncomfortable moments become easier to navigate. Your capacity for joy, connection, and self-trust grows bit by bit.

Recall a time—maybe recently—when you managed to surprise yourself by growing or changing, even if it was tiny. Did you set a boundary? Did you admit you were struggling? Did you laugh or let yourself rest without guilt? These moments count more than you think. Write down one way you've changed or grown since your trauma, no matter how small it seems right now.

You are not unfixable or defective. You're human—adaptable, resilient, worthy of every chance to reclaim yourself. Progress might be slow or uneven; it might sometimes look like two steps back for every one forward. But if there's even one spark of hope left in you—one moment where you question the voice that says "too broken"—that's enough to begin building something new from the inside out.

Shame, Blame, and the Silent Burdens of Recovery

Shame and self-blame often settle in quietly, gradually coloring your view of yourself and your world. You might catch yourself with thoughts like, "I should have known better," or "This is all my fault." Such thoughts linger, making it harder to seek help or even admit how you feel. Shame whispers that you are inherently flawed or unworthy, while blame convinces you you're at fault for your pain or for others' discomfort. This silent weight can make you shrink in conversations, apologize unnecessarily, or take on responsibility for others' moods.

The distinction between shame and guilt matters to your healing. Guilt signals, "I did something wrong," focusing on actions that can often be repaired. Shame, however, says, "I am wrong," targeting your core self and making you feel broken or unworthy. While guilt may ease once you address what happened, shame lingers and grows, thriving in vulnerability or exposure. For instance, forgetting a friend's birthday might make you feel guilty. But deciding you're a terrible friend unworthy of love—that's shame taking hold.

Trauma often teaches people to absorb blame for things they can't control, a habit that shows up in frequent apologizing, seeking to keep the peace, or feeling responsible for others' comfort. I once knew someone who apologized for everything—even when others erred or were upset. She described feeling as if she were "walking on eggshells," scanning constantly for potential faults—reflecting a learned response from years of misplaced blame.

Over time, this cycle of internalized blame becomes automatic. Maybe you obsess over past conversations, are anxious about missteps, or shrink back when faced with anger. These patterns usually take root in difficult childhoods or past relationships where you were made to feel responsible for the pain of others. Eventually, such habits mold how you see yourself; you might believe you're undeserving of kindness or that your needs are a burden.

Breaking through shame and blame isn't easy, but it starts with awareness. Notice when these feelings emerge, like after a tough work meeting or a disagreement. Naming shame aloud—even just to yourself—can diminish its power: "This is shame talking." Next, counter the inner critic with compassion. When you think, "I'm a failure," try, "I'm struggling, but that doesn't mean I'm broken." This isn't fake positivity; it's creating space between your identity and shame's narrative.

A helpful exercise is the "shame interrupter." When you spiral into self-blame, pause and think of what you'd say to a friend in your situation. Would you call them terrible or unworthy? Likely not. Offer yourself the same kindness: "You're having a hard time right now. That doesn't mean you're bad." Jot these phrases down as reminders for when your inner critic appears.

Simple Affirmations for Overwhelming Self-Blame

- I am allowed to make mistakes without losing my worth.
- My feelings are valid, even if others don't understand them.
- Needing help does not mean I am weak.
- I am learning and growing at my own pace.
- One moment or mistake does not define my entire self.

These statements won't erase shame overnight, but repeating them can gradually shift your inner narrative, softening the critical voice over time.

Pay attention when shame compels you to shrink, withdraw from friends, avoid eye contact, or go silent when hurt. These actions are signs that shame is influencing you. Naming these feelings—"I want to disappear right now because I feel ashamed"—makes them less overwhelming and gives you some control.

Take a moment to reflect: When do you most want to hide? What triggers your urge to shrink or apologize for just being? And—what helps you feel even a little safer? It could be reaching out to a trusted friend, taking a walk, or reminding yourself it's okay to take up space.

Shame and self-blame thrive in secrecy and silence. By noticing, naming, and replacing them with gentle compassion, even in small ways, you weaken their hold. You aren't alone—many others have learned to interrupt shame's narrative and replace it with one rooted in kindness and truth.

Remember this: naming your pain is a radical act of self-respect. The beliefs that kept you silent or small do not have to define you. In the next chapter, we'll explore practical steps for reconnecting with your real identity—one grounded in understanding, not in old stories or silent burdens.

Shame cast a long shadow over my life, leaving me with the persistent belief that I was fundamentally flawed, that everything about me was somehow wrong. Much of this deep-seated shame grew from my experiences in a strict, legalistic church environment during my childhood. When I became a parent myself, I realized how harmful these beliefs could be—not just for me, but for my children as well. I knew I wanted to offer them a sense of acceptance and worthiness that I had missed. This realization sparked my journey to rediscover my true identity through a new lens. As I turned to Scripture, I found reassurance in the message that I am chosen, loved, and cherished by God. Again and again, I encountered reminders that I am wanted and that His thoughts toward me are good. This truth became a powerful foundation for healing, gently challenging the shame I once carried.

3. Obstacles and Objections on the Healing Path

"I've Tried Everything"—Why Past Solutions Fell Short

You might be picking up this book thinking, "Here we go again," discouraged by shelves of self-help books and half-finished journals. Maybe you've joined groups, tried meditation apps, or made daily gratitude lists, only to end up more alone, frustrated, or ashamed when nothing stuck. This kind of exhaustion—heavy in your chest—can make healing feel like an empty promise. After chasing hope that fades, every attempt that doesn't work threatens to turn disappointment into hopelessness.

It's easy to blame yourself and wonder if you're not trying hard enough, or if you're just meant to feel this way forever. But this isn't a personal failure. Most solutions weren't designed for the complexity of trauma recovery. Many self-help books gloss over the deep impact trauma has on your mind and body, offering quick fixes like positive thinking or checklist routines, as if that could unravel years of survival wiring. Trauma isn't solved that way. These approaches rarely acknowledge how trauma disrupts your sense of safety, or the way your nervous system sometimes shuts down emotions to protect you. Some programs push rigid routines, shaming you for missing a day or falling behind—making you feel unsupported and even more certain you're not cut out for recovery.

A key reason many efforts fall flat is that they're one-size-fits-all. Healing after trauma isn't a recipe you follow—it's a process of listening to your own body after years of ignoring its signals. If a method doesn't fit your unique rhythm, comfort level, or readiness, it probably won't work for you. Many resources also ignore how crucial your body is to recovery. They focus only on changing thoughts, without addressing physical signs like tense muscles from anxiety or shortened breath when you're triggered. But trauma is held in the body as much as it is in memory. Ignoring this leaves out half of what's needed to heal.

Think about what you've tried before. Did those strategies push you through discomfort without honoring your limits? Did they offer real compassion for setbacks, or did they treat every pause as a failure? Were they flexible enough for you to take a break or slow down when life got hard? Maybe what was missing wasn't effort or motivation, but a sense of safety—a space where you could rest, free from shame and pressure.

Reflection Prompt: What Was Missing?

Take a moment to write down the approaches you've tried—books, groups, routines, or advice. For each, note what helped (even briefly) and what left you stuck or ashamed. Ask: "What did I need from those tools that I didn't get?" Maybe you needed more permission to rest, space to acknowledge setbacks, or a chance to be honest about where you really were.

Failed attempts don't mean healing is out of reach. They are data—clues about what supports you and what doesn't work for your nervous system. Each time a method failed, you learned something about your recovery style and needs. If a group was too fast, perhaps you need gentle steps and time to pause. If journaling didn't help, but music brought comfort, note that.

So-called "failure" usually means the method was wrong for you—not that you're wrong for needing something different. Your experiences deserve to be respected and learned from. Don't erase disappointments; look to them as guideposts for a more compassionate and personalized approach.

Healing isn't about perfectly following someone else's plan—it's about honoring both your pain and your resilience. When you reflect on the places you've felt stuck, consider them as part of your self-discovery, not proof you can't heal.

In my own journey, I tried everything I could think of—therapy, church, self-help books, and even avoidance—yet I often ended up feeling even more confused, hurt, and let down by others. Eventually, I realized I needed to step back and look for a different path to healing. It was then that I turned to God, honestly asking for guidance about what I truly needed. I sensed that what I was missing most was truth—a firm foundation I could trust. I chose to seek out that truth in God's word. Immersing myself in scripture, I began to ask deeper questions: Who is God, really? Who does He say I am? What does He promise? Dare I hope for a future with Him? This search for truth anchored me, providing clarity and comfort when everything else felt uncertain.

"What If This Makes Things Worse?"—Gentle Ways to Begin

It's natural to hesitate before looking closer at old wounds. You might worry that poking around in your history or talking about what hurts could make things unravel or even push you deeper into pain. This fear isn't weakness; it's wisdom. Your body and mind want to keep you safe. You've learned, maybe the hard way, that too much too fast can leave you raw or shaken. There's nothing wrong with wanting to protect yourself. Readiness, pacing, and a sense of safety matter more than any outside advice, and you deserve to approach healing at a rate that matches your comfort.

You don't have to jump in with both feet. There are gentle, "low-stakes" ways to begin exploring your identity and your story. Sometimes just noticing one thing that feels good or safe in your day—a warm mug, sunlight through the window, the sound of music—can be a quiet form of recovery. Sensory grounding offers practical entry points: try running your hands under cool water and describing the sensation, or look around and name three things in the room that seem comforting or familiar. Even pausing for a slow, two-minute breath—feeling the air move in, then out—can anchor you right here, right now. Micro-practices like these don't ask you to revisit trauma; they help your nervous system find calm and remind your body that safety is possible, even for a moment.

You might find it helpful to sketch out a personal "Safety Plan" for those times when life feels overwhelming or emotions spike out of nowhere. One easy way is to create a "red light/yellow light/green light" chart for your emotional states. In the green zone, you feel steady or hopeful; yellow might mean you're anxious, irritable, or tired but still able to function; red means you're flooded, panicking, or numb. Next to each color, list a few actions or soothers: maybe texting a trusted friend, playing your favorite song, cuddling with a pet, or simply stepping outside for fresh air. When things get rough, this chart acts as a quick guide—a reminder that you have options and don't need to think through everything when overwhelmed.

You never have to force yourself through this material or push past your limits. Sometimes you'll read a page and feel okay; other times, it may sting or bring up more than you expected. That's not failure—it's information from your body about what feels safe right now. Permission to pause is always on the table. Skipping ahead or putting the book down for a while is not proof of avoidance or weakness. You can always come back when you feel steadier.

Sidebar: Permission to Pause

You are allowed to move at whatever pace fits your needs. Healing isn't about sticking to someone else's timeline. If something feels too much, set it aside. Skipping sections or returning later is not failing—it's respecting your boundaries.

Consider trying "name three safe things in the room" as a soft entry point when anxiety spikes or old memories surface unexpectedly. For some folks, gentle touch—holding your own hand, wrapping up in a favorite blanket—brings grounding. Others use breathwork: inhale slowly for four counts, hold for four, then exhale for six. Notice if anything shifts inside—maybe just a little more space.

Building safety means knowing you can step back anytime things get too intense. If you sense overwhelm rising, use your chart or list of soothers before continuing. Over time, these small acts of self-kindness help your nervous system learn that exploring identity and healing don't have to mean losing control.

The process of reclaiming yourself after trauma isn't a race or a test of endurance. It's more like learning to swim in shallow water before venturing farther out. Gentle beginnings count just as much as bold leaps. You're the expert on what pace feels right for you—trust that wisdom as you move forward.

"My Trauma Is Different"—Honoring Diversity in Healing

No two stories of pain look exactly alike. Your experience is singular; it can't be captured by anyone else's script. Maybe you survived a sudden loss, or perhaps your heart carries years of microaggressions that few around you ever noticed. Some wounds are loud and obvious, while others live quietly beneath the surface, shaped by the culture, family, or faith you grew up in. I've listened to friends and clients who sometimes whisper, "I just don't see myself in any of these books. My story doesn't fit." You might feel that too—like your pain is out of place, or your background makes healing even more complicated. That sense is valid.

Consider a few voices: A Black woman from the South who shared, "In my community, we don't talk about therapy. Admitting I needed help felt like betraying my family." A queer teenager who said, "Hiding who I was from everyone—even myself—left scars I couldn't see until I was older." An immigrant father recalls, "I lost my language and my roots. Grief wasn't just about what happened to me—it was what I left behind." Another voice, a middle-aged man whose trauma came from generational silence: "My father taught me boys don't cry. So I stopped sharing anything real, even with myself." Each describes a different kind of pain, shaped by race, gender, faith, or the weight of family legacy.

Our identities—how we see ourselves in terms of culture, gender, age, spirituality—shape not only how we experience trauma but also what healing looks like. For readers who identify as BIPOC (Black, Indigenous, People of Color), trauma may be tangled with racism or cultural expectations that silence suffering. For LGBTQ+ folks, identity wounds can come from both outside rejection and internalized shame. Immigrants may face the grief of losing their homeland or language, carrying old traditions while trying to fit into new norms. Generational trauma—the kind passed down through families—can make it hard to even recognize where your own pain ends and your ancestors' begins. Sometimes faith is a shield; other times, it's a source of conflict or shame, especially when communities use spirituality to judge instead of support.

If you've ever felt like self-help advice just doesn't land for you, that's not your fault. Many recovery tools weren't written with all backgrounds in mind. The affirmations may not match your spiritual language. Some exercises might ask you to picture "safe spaces" that never existed for you. The advice to talk openly may bump up against family rules of silence or pride. And sometimes what "works" for one group feels empty—or even harmful—to another.

The beautiful thing is that healing isn't about following a rigid template. You have permission to adapt every exercise in this book to fit your reality. Replace affirmations with words from your own language or faith tradition. If certain prompts don't resonate, swap them out for questions that feel true for you. If a practice feels off or lands wrong, trust that instinct and reshape it. Maybe your rituals include prayer, lighting a candle, or singing an old song—those count just as much as any tool offered here. Sometimes finding a therapist who shares your background or values can make all the difference; other times, connecting with community groups or elders offers support that feels more authentic.

Make It Yours: Customizing Your Healing

Try this: When you come across an exercise or prompt in this book, pause and ask yourself, "How would this sound in my own words—or in my family's way?" Jot down alternative phrases or rituals that feel safe and real to you. Lean into music, poetry, or spiritual texts from your heritage if they comfort you more than standard affirmations.

You are the expert on your own experience. That isn't just a slogan—it's the foundation for lasting change. Trust your gut about what helps and what doesn't. If you wonder how to honor the uniqueness of your story as you read, start by noticing which parts of your history want to be seen and which need gentleness right now. Give yourself the freedom to heal in ways that fit you—not someone else's idea of what recovery "should" look like.

"I'm Not Ready for Therapy"—Gentle Self-Exploration Tools

There are so many reasons you might not feel ready to sit across from a therapist. Sometimes it's the price tag that makes therapy out of reach, especially when you're juggling bills and daily stress. Maybe it's the ache of stigma—fear of being judged, misunderstood, or labeled. Some people have had bad experiences with professionals in the past, which can leave a bitter taste and a wall of distrust. For others, just talking about what happened feels impossible. Even the idea of opening up can trigger a wave of overwhelm that's hard to shake. Sometimes you don't even know where to start or what to say. And some cultures, families, or communities simply don't see therapy as an option or a safe space. If any of this sounds familiar, please know that it's okay. Not wanting to start therapy right now—or ever—doesn't mean you don't care about healing.

You still deserve tools that can help you reconnect with yourself in ways that feel safe and private. There are trauma-informed approaches that don't require you to bare your soul to another person or push past your comfort zone. One gentle starting point is grounding—simple techniques that bring your focus back to the present moment. The 5-4-3-2-1 senses method is a favorite among trauma survivors and therapists alike: pause, look around, and name five things you can see, four things you can touch, three sounds you can hear, two scents you can smell, and one taste in your mouth. This exercise roots you in the here and now, calming anxious thoughts and helping your mind and body feel more connected.

Exploring who you are doesn't have to mean digging into pain right away. You can start with something as basic as making lists—no pressure, just curiosity. Write down foods you enjoy, colors you like, places that feel comfortable, or even memories that bring a small sense of peace. Try jotting down values that matter to you: kindness, honesty, creativity, humor, faith—whatever rings true. These lists don't have to be deep or perfect. They're a starting point for rediscovering the parts of yourself that trauma might have muted.

Creative outlets can offer another route into self-discovery without triggering old memories. Art doesn't judge spelling or grammar. Drawing a picture of a place that feels safe—a beach, a childhood bedroom, a favorite café—can be more revealing than any written journal entry. If words are hard, let music do the talking. Build a playlist of songs that calm or uplift you, then notice how your body reacts when you listen. Movement helps too. A walk around the block or gentle stretching while breathing deeply can help loosen emotional knots without forcing you to analyze them.

Sometimes reflection feels safer with non-threatening prompts. "What colors make me feel calm?" "What would my perfect day look like if stress weren't an issue?" "Which activities leave me feeling lighter, even just for a moment?" Keep these questions light and simple if heavy ones send your mind spinning. The goal isn't to dig up pain, but to dip a toe in the water of self-awareness—slowly, gently.

It's also important to know when self-help isn't enough. If you notice that sadness or fear won't lift for weeks on end or if daily life becomes impossible—maybe you can't get out of bed, take care of yourself, or handle basic responsibilities—it's time to pause and consider reaching out for more support. Red flags include thoughts of hurting yourself or others that won't go away, panic attacks that leave you feeling out of control, or distress that keeps building no matter what you try. These are signs that professional support might be necessary for your safety and well-being.

Support Scale Check-In

On a scale from 1 (barely coping) to 10 (feeling mostly steady), where do you land today? Jot down that number and think about what would help move you half a point higher—maybe it's calling someone safe, making a doctor's appointment, or simply resting without guilt.

Gentle self-exploration doesn't require expertise or bravery beyond your current capacity—just small, honest steps toward understanding yourself again. Each step counts, no matter how tiny it feels.

"I Don't Have Time or Energy"—Micro-Wins for Busy Lives

If you're flipping through these pages at the end of a long shift, after wrangling kids, or squeezing in a moment between caring for someone else and just trying to get by, I see you. The weight of real life can feel relentless. You might feel like your to-do list grows faster than you can cross things off, and healing your identity gets buried under the mess and noise of survival. Sometimes, the idea of "working on yourself" sounds impossible when you barely have time to breathe. It's so common to feel like you're falling short before you even start. The shame spiral can sneak up—whispering that you never do enough, or that recovery is just for people with luxury or endless hours. You're not lazy or failing. You're simply stretched thin in ways that get overlooked.

Healing doesn't demand sweeping changes or hours of meditation. In fact, the smallest actions—what I call micro-wins—can have remarkable power. These are tiny, doable acts that nudge your healing forward, even when your energy is spent or your motivation has worn thin. Imagine pressing pause on the chaos for just thirty seconds to notice your breath—a true act of self-respect. A quick text to a friend, sharing even a silly meme or a simple "thinking of you," counts as a connection. Or maybe you just sit quietly for a moment and try to name what you're feeling—tired, hopeful, angry, numb. That's progress. Each of these small moves signals to your mind and body that you matter, even in the busiest seasons.

Micro-practices fit into the jagged edges of real life. If you've got one minute—stand by the window and notice the color of the sky, take three deep breaths, or unclench your jaw. If five minutes open up—pull out a notepad and scribble three words that capture your mood, stretch your arms over your head and roll your shoulders, or listen to one song that lifts your spirit. On days when even thinking feels hard, turn on an uplifting playlist while folding laundry, let sunlight hit your face for half a minute, or splash cold water on your wrists. These tiny gestures soothe your nervous system without requiring much thought.

You can even tailor your micro-wins to match how much energy you have. Low motivation? Just lie down and notice how the fabric feels against your skin for ten seconds. Moderate energy? Try writing a single sentence about something that didn't go wrong today. Feeling slightly more up for it? Step outside and notice three sounds around you—traffic, birds, the hum of a neighbor's lawnmower. There's no wrong way to approach this. Every action is valid.

Tracking these micro-wins helps build hope and momentum—you might be surprised how quickly they stack up. A simple visual tracker can work wonders: make a grid for each day of the week and add a checkmark whenever you do something that honors your healing, no matter how small. At the end of the week, look back and see those marks as proof of your effort and resilience—not as grades, but as reminders that you are moving forward despite everything else demanding your attention.

Reflection Prompt: Noticing Your Micro-Wins

Pause and ask: What is one thing—no matter how tiny—that I did today to support myself? Maybe it was drinking water with intention, saying "no" once, or simply acknowledging a hard feeling without judging it.

Small wins aren't insignificant—they are building blocks for reclaiming identity in the middle of real life. When your energy is low and demands are high, these moments matter more than ever. Micro-wins remind you that healing belongs in every life, not just in quiet retreats or perfect routines.

Remember this: progress is made up of many small steps, not giant leaps. You don't need more hours in the day to start reclaiming yourself; every micro-win is a sign that hope is alive. Up next, we'll look at ways to reconnect with who you really are—even if that sense feels far away right now.

Journaling became a cornerstone of my healing journey. I found comfort in writing out my prayers, using these moments to honestly express my thoughts and emotions, and then quietly listening for God's gentle guidance. During especially stressful times, I incorporated tapping and EMDR techniques, which allowed me to work through painful memories in a safe and structured way. Partnering with an EMDR therapist helped me process experiences I once believed were impossible to face. These small, consistent steps gently challenged the limiting beliefs I held about myself, gradually uncovering and restoring the identity that was always meant for me.

4. Mapping the Journey

The Identity Reconstruction Roadmap

Your Identity Compass: Pinpointing Where You Are Now

Sometimes you wake up and feel unsure of how you ended up where you are, or even what "here" really means. Maybe scrolling through your phone feels empty, and nothing excites you as it used to. This kind of lostness isn't about geography—it's about feeling disconnected from yourself, often after trauma has shaken your inner compass. Understanding where you stand in your sense of self is essential before you can move forward. This section will help you gently and honestly ask yourself: Where am I, right now, with myself?

Start with a practical self-inventory—there's no scoring, and it isn't a test. The "Where Am I Now?" worksheet is for your eyes only. Use any notebook or notes app. Reflect on these five areas: God, values, interests, boundaries, relationships, and self-trust. For each, jot down a few honest thoughts about what feels true now. If you're unsure about your values or don't find anything interesting, that's okay—write that down. Even naming confusion is a powerful first step. Don't make it sound better than it is; honesty is more helpful. If numbness is the only thing you feel right now, note it. "I'm not sure" is an honest place to start.

God: Who is he? Do I trust him?

Values: Write what matters to you now or what used to matter. **Interests:** List hobbies or things that once excited you or still do. **Boundaries:** Consider where you say yes or no—has that shifted?

Relationships: Note who feels supportive versus draining. **Self-trust:** Ask if you trust your gut or find yourself always second-guessing.

You're not aiming for perfect answers, just an honest picture of where you are. Imagine this not as a checklist, but a wheel—a spectrum. On one end is "lost": feeling disconnected and foggy about who you are. Next is "questioning": noticing something's off and wondering what's missing. Then comes "experimenting": trying out small changes to see what feels right. Finally, "reconnecting": glimpses of recognizing yourself again. Most people move among these over time; it's not fixed.

It's common to focus on what feels broken, but remember to look for strengths too. Even on tough days, you handle more than you realize. Try a quick "Strengths Snapshot" from the past week: maybe you supported a friend, managed to get out of bed, made a meal, paid a bill, or got through a difficult day. Write down at least two ways you showed up for yourself, even in small ways. Don't dismiss so-called ordinary victories.

Often, resilience is in answering one difficult email or asking for help when you need it. Pushing through when motivation is low or anxiety is high takes strength. If you can't think of recent examples, recall past times you surprised yourself with resourcefulness or courage—even if long ago.

Wherever you are on this compass is valid. Maybe you feel deep confusion, or maybe you're only starting to have glimmers of self-awareness. All of it counts, and none of it means you're failing or behind. Healing isn't linear, and there's no timetable for rediscovering yourself after trauma (APA list: 18). Some days you'll leap forward;

others may look stagnant. Recognizing your true location is an act of courage.

Reflection Exercise: Your Identity Compass

Spend ten minutes journaling these prompts:

- What do I value most right now? What did I value in the past?
- Which interests or passions still attract me? Which feel out of reach?
- Where have I set boundaries lately? Where are boundaries missing?
- Who in my life supports me? Who drains me?
- Do I trust my feelings and decisions? When do I doubt myself most?
- What do I want to say to God?

Next, sketch a wheel with four sections: Lost, Questioning, Experimenting, Reconnecting. For each area above, place a dot in the section that best represents where you currently stand.

Revisit this compass regularly—weekly, monthly, or anytime strong feelings emerge. Your answers and positions will change as you grow and try out new ways of being.

If you find yourself comparing your progress to others', pause: you are not behind. You're exactly where you need to be right now. Pay attention to your unique strengths, and jot down any shifts or small changes in the margins of this book or your own journal—they matter.

Use this compass as your personal check-in tool as you move through the book. It will help you notice growth that could go unseen and guide you back if you feel lost along the way.

Setting Your Own Pace—A "Choose-Your-Own-Healing" Model

Healing from trauma isn't a straight path; it's more like wandering through winding trails with many options. Some days you might be ready to move forward, while other days, you may need to pause or take a detour. You don't need to match anyone else's pace or force yourself onto a timeline that doesn't fit. Listen to your own body and mind—sometimes you'll be energized and open to new things, while at other times, even small steps will feel overwhelming. This isn't a setback—it's your body asking for what it needs.

Consider the chapters and exercises in this book as options on a map. Some will suit you now, others later, and some never. There's no required order—choose the sections or practices that speak to you and skip or revisit others. Think of it as a menu to sample rather than a list to complete. Maybe today you read about boundaries, next week you try a grounding exercise, or later, you move ahead to future-planning because that feels relevant. Choose what resonates, and leave the rest.

It's normal—and encouraged—to pause, skip, or revisit sections as you need. Healing isn't measured by speed or by completing every exercise. If a chapter feels too heavy, step away and return later, or not at all. Some people find writing helpful; others might prefer movement or art. Maybe a walk helps more than journaling at this moment. That's perfectly valid. If you notice pressure to "keep up," remind yourself: it's okay to read one paragraph a day or none at all for a while.

Sidebar: It's Okay to Take Breaks

If you're feeling overwhelmed or numb, take a break—drink some water, watch something light, call a friend, or just relax. There's no race, and burnout gets you nowhere.

As you go through these chapters, consider building your own healing toolkit. Jot down the strategies that feel helpful, neutral, or uncomfortable. Maybe drawing helps more than writing; maybe guided meditations aren't your thing, but stretching works well. Keep notes in the margins or in a separate notebook about what feels comforting, what doesn't, and what's in between. This toolkit should be tailored to your needs, not a copy of someone else's routine.

Everyone's toolkit will be different. One person may fill it with doodles and playlists, while another prefers index cards with kind reminders or prayers. If you prefer structure, organize your notes by themes like boundaries, self-soothing, connection, and hope. If you hate structure, keep it messy. The important thing is that your toolkit is real for you.

Set micro-goals based on your actual energy and motivation, not what you think you "should" do. Maybe today's goal is simply reading a page or doing one reflection. It could be sending a supportive text or spending two minutes focusing on your breath before bed. Perhaps it's stepping outside for five slow breaths or noticing something that feels safe. Small goals are just as crucial as bigger milestones—they build momentum and show that progress can happen in tiny, everyday steps.

Some sample micro-goals:

- "I'll read one paragraph today."

- "I'll try a new grounding technique this week."
- "I'll write down three things I did right today—even if they're small."
- "I'll listen to mood-lifting music for five minutes tonight."
- "If I feel anxious, I'll name three things I see around me."

If visual reminders help, make a "Pace Yourself" card and put it somewhere you'll see it, or set phone reminders like "Slow progress counts" or "Resting is part of healing."

Adjust or skip anything in this book to fit your pace. If something doesn't feel right, trust yourself to change or ignore it for now. For example, one reader preferred making playlists to journaling, using music to reflect on emotions. Another walked while squeezing a stress ball instead of sitting still to process feelings. There is no wrong way—as long as you're listening to yourself.

Every choice teaches you something about what helps you heal. Honor your own capacity, and celebrate every step, big or small. The heart of recovery is listening inward, following what fits, and trusting that something positive is happening, even if progress is slow or hard to see.

Visual Progress Trackers: Marking Micro-Steps Forward

Healing after trauma can feel invisible. You put in work and try new things, and sometimes it just seems like nothing changes. Days blur together, and you wonder if you're actually moving forward at all. That's where visual progress tracking becomes a game-changer. When you have something you can see and touch—a chart, a coloring page, a checklist on the fridge—it gives shape to the invisible work you're doing. Suddenly, those tiny wins aren't lost in the shuffle. They show up, real and unmistakable, right in front of you.

You don't need fancy tools to get started. Use any notebook, calendar, or blank sheet of paper. Some folks love printable trackers with boxes to tick or doodle in. Others sketch their own, coloring a square for each day they meet a goal or try something new. There's something satisfying about shading a box, adding a sticker, or just scribbling a simple "yes" on a calendar. It's a tactile reward for effort that often goes unnoticed.

Seeing your own progress does more than just boost motivation—it helps your brain recognize and celebrate forward movement, even when it's slow. Psychologists call this "behavioral activation," which is just a fancy way of saying that marking small wins builds hope and keeps you going on hard days (APA list: 17). The act itself—making your effort visible—signals to your nervous system that change is happening, even when you don't feel it yet. When you look back and notice more colored boxes or fewer blank days, it gives real proof that your actions matter.

You can track almost anything related to reclaiming your sense of self. Emotional growth might mean noting days when you recognize a feeling or name an emotion out loud. For those who struggle with relationships, you might log every time you reach out to someone or resist old patterns in difficult conversations. If you're working on body awareness or somatic healing, try a "body check-in" tracker—mark each day you do a grounding exercise or move your body in a way that feels safe. Cognitive growth could involve tracking days when you challenge a negative thought or try a new perspective in your self-talk.

Mood meters are one of my favorite tools for this kind of work. Draw a basic chart with days across the top and different feelings down the side—connected, hopeful, numb, anxious, curious. Each evening, mark where you land. Over weeks or months, you'll spot trends: maybe numbness fades as connection grows, or perhaps hard days show up less often than before. Sometimes it's as simple as writing one word for each day—"steady," "lost," "okay," "hopeful." No need for perfection; the act of marking it down is what counts.

Wins logs are equally powerful. Keep a space—maybe in your tracker or a separate notebook—to jot down micro-wins each day or week. They don't have to be dramatic. "I made myself breakfast instead of skipping." "I said no when I needed to." "I listened to my gut and took a break." "I noticed when my anxiety started and paused before reacting." Each entry is evidence of growth, no matter how minor it looks on paper.

Trying new things deserves its own tracker too—especially for those who feel stuck in routine or numbness. Make a list of self-care ideas, hobbies, foods, or routines to experiment with. Each time you try something—even if you don't love it—mark it down. Over time, this builds a sense of agency and curiosity about what might bring color back into life.

It's easy to dismiss these tiny steps as "not enough." But every time you mark a box or write down a win, you send yourself the message: tiny is mighty. The smallest shift—a moment of self-kindness, an extra breath before reacting is worth real celebration. Don't wait for big breakthroughs to acknowledge yourself.

A young girl I know uses mood meters and micro-wins logs. She had felt stuck for years—until she flipped back through her tracker and saw that her "bad days" were actually getting fewer and farther between. The visual proof helped her believe change was happening even when her feelings wavered day-to-day.

Imagine someone named Dev who struggled with feeling disconnected from his body after trauma. He created a simple chart: every day, he did a grounding exercise (even two minutes of feeling his feet on the floor), he colored one square blue. Six weeks later, he had more blue than white—and realized he was connecting more often than not for the first time in years.

Sidebar: If You Fall Off, Just Start Again

Progress isn't erased by missed days or setbacks. If your tracker goes blank for a week (or longer), start fresh without guilt. Every return is still part of your healing.

These visual tools exist to support you—not to judge or grade your progress. Think of them as gentle reminders that no step is too small to count. Whether you use color, stickers, checkmarks, or words, celebrate each mark as real evidence of your effort and resilience.

Normalizing Detours: Why Setbacks Aren't Failure

If you've ever felt like you were finally making progress, only to wake up one morning back in old habits or flooded by anxiety, you're not broken. This isn't a sign that you're failing. In trauma recovery, the path is rarely straight or smooth. Sometimes, it zigzags. Growth can look a lot like a spiral—each loop brings you back to familiar territory, but with a little more wisdom each time around. That's not going backward; it's circling through layers of healing. Expecting yourself to only move forward sets you up for disappointment and shame. When you encounter a setback or a stretch where nothing seems to change, remind yourself: this is normal. You may notice periods where things feel lighter, then suddenly find yourself overwhelmed by self-doubt, isolation, or even old coping strategies that you thought you'd left behind. These "relapses" aren't failures—they're natural responses when life throws something new or hard your way.

It's easy to get discouraged during these times. You might catch yourself thinking, "I should be past this," or "Why can't I just move on?" But if you zoom out, those detours often reveal something important about what still needs care or attention. Maybe you visit family and old wounds flare up, or a stressful week at work brings back anxious habits. Instead of seeing these moments as proof that nothing's changed, try viewing them as messengers. They're showing you where pain lives in your body or where boundaries need strengthening. For example, one friend shared how a weekend with relatives left her feeling raw and shut down for days. At first, she called it a failure, but as she reflected, she realized those feelings pointed straight to a boundary she'd been ignoring. That realization led her to practice saying "no" more firmly next time—and that's real growth.

So when you notice yourself slipping into old patterns, ask gently: "What is this detour trying to tell me about my needs?" Maybe you needed more rest, more space, or more support than you thought. Notice the urge to pile on shame and instead try curiosity. You might find that a setback is actually a sign your system is working hard to protect you from overwhelm. Sometimes anxiety spikes because your body is warning you about an unsafe situation—or reminding you of something unresolved. Rather than fighting that response, get curious about what triggered it.

Responding to setbacks with compassion changes everything. When you catch yourself spiraling into self-blame, try saying out loud (or writing down), "This is part of healing, not proof that I'm failing." Another helpful script: "Setbacks are information, not condemnation." If shame creeps in, pause and imagine what you'd say to a friend who's struggling—most likely, it wouldn't be harsh or critical; it would be gentle and kind.

Practical strategies help too. If you feel derailed, grounding techniques can anchor you back in the present and reduce the emotional charge of a setback. One simple approach is the "5-4-3-2-1" method: name five things you see, four things you feel (touch), three sounds you hear, two scents you smell, and one taste in your mouth. This pulls your focus away from spiraling thoughts and reconnects you with your body and surroundings. Another option is deep breathing—inhale slowly for four counts, hold for two, exhale for six. Or try gentle movement: stand up, roll your shoulders, walk around the room for a minute. These resets aren't magic fixes, but they interrupt the shame cycle and create space for reflection.

Instead of pretending setbacks didn't happen, honor them in your progress tracker or journal. Give them their own color or symbol—maybe a squiggly line for detour days or a cloud for stormy feelings. Documenting these moments acknowledges that healing isn't all sunny skies; sometimes clouds roll through, but that doesn't erase your previous progress. In fact, survivors who track setbacks often notice they bounce back quicker and learn more each time.

Consider Maya's story. After several calm weeks, she had a full-blown panic attack before a doctor's appointment—a trigger she thought she'd conquered. At first, she felt defeated. But after marking the day in her tracker and writing about it that evening, she realized her body was reacting to memories of feeling powerless in medical settings as a child. That awareness helped her plan better boundaries for her next visit. Her detour became a source of insight instead of just pain.

As you continue mapping your growth, remember that every spiral or zigzag is another layer of wisdom and resilience forming beneath the surface. With each return to old patterns, you have new tools and understanding to bring with you. The process might be unpredictable and sometimes frustrating, but it's real—and it's yours.

Remember this: recovery isn't about never stumbling again; it's about getting up (or even just pausing) with more self-acceptance than last time. Each detour offers clues about what needs care next. As you move forward into reconnecting with your authentic self in the next chapter, bring this knowledge: setbacks are not dead ends—they're signposts along the way to something more honest and whole.

One of the most effective methods I've found for staying connected to my sense of self is Bible art journaling. During my cancer treatments, I continued a practice of reading a Psalm and then writing my thoughts, prayers, and reflections in the margins of my Bible. This simple act became an anchor for me—helping me process my fears and emotions in a tangible way. Now, when anxiety creeps in—whether it's worry about a follow-up appointment or fear of the cancer returning—I revisit those same passages. Seeing how God guided me through that difficult time provides reassurance, grounding me in the truth of His faithfulness and reminding me just how far I've come.

5. Reconnecting with the Authentic Self

Rediscovering "Likes" and "Dislikes" After Years of Numbness

Have you ever stood in front of vending machines or stared at a menu, feeling unsure of what you want, choices that once felt simple suddenly paralyzing? If so, you're not alone. Trauma often creates "preference amnesia"—your favorite snack, color, or even go-to coffee order fading into uncertainty. This is a natural, protective response to being overwhelmed and survival mode, not a character flaw or laziness.

When traumatized, your brain shifts into survival, focusing on just making it through. Preferences—those unique quirks that made you feel like yourself—fade as staying safe takes priority. Suddenly, everyday choices feel enormous. It's like being a kid in the ice cream aisle, but excitement is replaced by a fog: nothing stands out. You may find yourself saying, "I don't care," not because you truly don't, but because those parts of you have grown quiet.

This is your nervous system protecting you—muting desires in case they might bring disappointment or loss. The good news is those parts aren't gone. They're just dormant. With patience and gentle curiosity, you can coax them back.

So where do you begin? Start small. Try the "One Small Thing" prompt: over the next day, pay attention to the tiniest flickers of preference. Notice if you reach for tea instead of water, if certain music draws you in, or if you choose a blue pen over a black one. Your instincts might whisper that you'd rather sit in the sun than in the shade. These micro-preferences matter. You don't have to overhaul your life or immediately declare favorites—simply tune in to what attracts your attention or brings a hint of comfort.

If choices feel overwhelming, experiment in low-pressure situations. Order a new drink, or pick a random movie to watch. If it isn't perfect, that's okay. The goal isn't to find "the best," but to practice choosing for yourself, even in small ways. Over time, you'll likely find the simple act of making a choice—simply because you want to—can feel freeing.

Journaling or tracking can help make these rediscoveries more visible. No need for fancy tools—use sticky notes, phone memos, or scraps of paper. Write down discoveries as you notice them: "Today I liked warm socks better than bare feet," or "I preferred the smell of fresh bread to lavender." If you like structure, make a basic Likes/Dislikes table and jot down tiny discoveries every day. These small records are gentle proof that your preferences are still alive and ready to grow.

Remember, preferences change, and that's healthy—it means healing is happening. If you're uncertain about what you enjoy, it's a sign your mind is waking up from numbness, not failing. One survivor recalled her senses returning after years of bland meals: "Suddenly I craved spicy food—I hadn't wanted flavor since before my divorce. It was like rediscovering a part of myself." Another woman impulsively bought a bright yellow sweater after years of neutrals. "It felt strange, but also thrilling."

If you don't know what you want today, it doesn't mean you

never will. It just means the part of you that holds preferences is stretching its legs after being cramped. Allow yourself to be unsure. If you pick something and dislike it, that's still progress. It means you're paying attention.

Interactive Exercise: My Daily Preference Tracker

Create a chart with two columns: "Today I Liked" and "Today I Didn't Like." Try to fill at least one row daily for a week. Each evening, jot down even the smallest detail—maybe soft pajamas felt good, or you disliked background noise while working. There's no judgment—just gentle noticing.

If even this feels like pressure, keep it light. Some days, your entry might say, "Nothing stood out," but that's fine. Return to it the next day without expectation.

Progress may be slow, and some days may yield no clear answers. Simply showing up for yourself, even in uncertainty, is courageous.

A survivor once shared about rediscovering flavor: "I enjoyed cinnamon toast again, and I cried—not because it was great toast, but because I realized I was still in there somewhere." Even if today feels gray and indecisive, by tuning in to the subtlest signals, you invite color and choice back—one flicker at a time.

Sidebar: If today brings no clarity, try again tomorrow. Every moment of curiosity plants a seed for your authentic self to return.

Values Inventory: What Truly Matters to You Now?

Trauma can make you feel like you're living on autopilot—

doing what's expected or seeking approval—while your real values fade into the background. Often, coping with difficult experiences means adapting to others' rules, suppressing your true self to keep the peace, or prioritizing survival over authenticity. This isn't a personal failing; it's a typical survival strategy when life has been overwhelming for too long.

Elena, an elderly woman, once realized she'd spent years chasing her family's ideals—hard work, silence, unquestioned tradition. She worked late at a job she disliked, avoided speaking up, and faked enjoyment of hobbies—just to keep the peace. The realization hit her after a tense family dinner: she didn't believe in many of the things she pursued. That moment held both relief and grief, but inspired her to begin discovering what actually mattered to her.

If this resonates with you, know it's normal for trauma to cloud your sense of what you value. But your values remain, even if they feel distant. With a bit of gentle reflection, you can uncover them again.

Here's a simple exercise to clarify your values. Start by scanning this list:

acceptance, adventure, authenticity, balance, beauty, belonging, compassion, connection, courage, creativity, curiosity, dependability, dignity, empathy, equality, faith, family, flexibility, forgiveness, freedom, generosity, gratitude, growth, honesty, hope, humor, integrity, joy, justice, kindness, learning, love, loyalty, openness, optimism, patience, peace, perseverance, playfulness, resilience, respect, responsibility, safety, security, self-expression, service, spirituality, stability, trust

Circle or write down five that stand out to you today. If you're unsure, start with ten and whittle down to five. Don't overthink it; curiosity is enough. If nothing feels right at first or you go blank, that's okay—just give yourself a moment.

Reflect on: "When did I feel most alive or 'right' in my past?" Maybe laughing with friends on a trip, volunteering, or comforting someone. Look for moments that brought warmth or pride, however small—they offer clues to your true values.

Now consider the present: What values do you want to live by now? Trauma can make you adopt survival-based values such as control ("If I keep everything perfect, I'll stay safe") or invisibility ("If I don't stand out, I won't be hurt"). These may have helped you cope but may not serve your authentic self today. You might sense a tug-of-war between old scripts and new desires—maybe you now want self-kindness over perfectionism, or adventure over always playing it safe.

Try drawing two columns—"Then" and "Now." Under "Then," jot down survival-driven values like silence over honesty, people-pleasing over self-respect, or security over growth. Under "Now," list what feels truer for you today: authenticity over approval, courage over comfort, learning over stagnation. There's no need to judge yourself if the past still has a hold; this step is about making room for new possibilities, not erasing history.

To bring these reflections into everyday life, set a "values intention" for the week. Keep it simple and honest: "This week, I'll notice when I want to choose peace over conflict and pause before reacting," or "I intend to value connection by reaching out to a friend." You might put your top value words on sticky notes or set reminders on your phone.

Exploring your values is an ongoing journey, not a one-time task. Sometimes old memories will bring up former values; sometimes you'll find new ones that surprise you. Let curiosity guide you, and allow your list to evolve with you.

If you run into confusion or resistance (like an inner critic telling you your values don't matter), pause and remember that uncertainty is part of growth. There's no deadline, and you aren't "behind." Every reflection brings you a bit closer to living from your authentic self, not someone else's expectations.

Even asking these questions can shift things inside. Naming what's important—even just for today—creates space for your true identity. Keep your values list handy and let it grow and change as you do. Tomorrow's answers may differ from today's—that's a sign of growth, not failure. Most importantly, know that honoring what matters, even in small ways, can begin to reshape how you move through the world.

Small Experiments: Safely Testing New and Old Interests

Trying something new, or even returning to an activity you once loved, can stir up a swarm of nerves and doubts after living through trauma. You might feel a strange mix of excitement and dread, or catch yourself thinking, "What if I can't enjoy this anymore? What if I try and fail?" This fear is real and totally understandable. Trauma often makes the world feel unpredictable. When your sense of self is shaken, even picking up an old paintbrush or signing up for a pottery class can feel risky, as if the stakes are impossibly high for something that should be simple.

I remember working with someone who used to adore painting. She kept her brushes packed away in a box for years, not because she didn't miss them, but because she was afraid that trying again would only remind her how much had changed. She said, "If I sit down and the spark isn't there, it'll just prove I've lost that part of me forever." That kind of fear can keep you stuck, circling old memories but never testing the waters. For her—and for so many others—the hardest part wasn't the blank canvas, but the possibility of disappointment.

But here's the thing: experimenting with interests doesn't have to be a big leap. In fact, the safest way to start is to shrink the experiment down until it feels nearly weightless. Think of it as "interest tasting"—sampling activities with zero pressure to commit. It could be doodling in the margins of your notebook for ten minutes, queuing up a song you've never heard before, or chopping veggies for a new recipe. Maybe you watch a documentary on a topic that's always piqued your curiosity, or you walk a different route home just to see what's there. The key is to make these experiments so small and low-risk that the outcome truly doesn't matter—success isn't about mastery or even enjoyment, but about giving yourself space to try.

Here's a menu of micro-experiments you might try:

- Sketch something simple, like your coffee mug or a leaf from outside, for just ten minutes.
- Listen to a genre of music you never thought you'd like—jazz, reggae, classical, lo-fi beats.
- Stir together a new sauce or bake an easy batch of cookies.

- Watch the first episode of a show outside your usual favorites.
- Visit a thrift shop or art supply store just to browse, no purchase required.
- Rearrange one shelf or corner in your living space.
- Write a silly poem or haiku—no one else has to read it.
- Try out a basic yoga video on YouTube or stretch in your living room.

These aren't meant to become permanent fixtures in your life. They're quick tests—ways to make contact with curiosity again. As you move through each experiment, pay close attention to what your body tells you. You might notice a tiny flutter of interest in your chest, a softening in your shoulders, or even mild irritation or boredom. All of these responses are information. There's no need to judge them as good or bad.

It helps to track not just what you did, but how it felt—before, during, and after. You might keep a little log: "Tried doodling for 10 minutes. Felt nervous at first, my hand was shaky. Five minutes in, lost track of time and noticed my breathing slowed down. Afterwards, felt proud I finished, even if the drawing was silly." Another day: "Listened to bluegrass music—honestly, it annoyed me after two songs. Not my thing." The point isn't to force yourself into enjoyment but to notice what lights anything up inside you—even if it's just a flicker.

Don't be surprised if some experiments bring up more anxiety than delight, or if boredom creeps in quickly. That's perfectly normal after trauma has pressed pause on your interests for a long time.

Sometimes you'll get halfway through an activity and want to quit—sometimes you should. Sticking it out isn't always brave; knowing when you're done is its own kind of wisdom.

You might find it helpful to chart your reactions for each experiment. Make three columns: Activity / What I Felt Before / What I Felt After. You might record "Cooking—anxious before, calm after," or "Watching nature documentary—neutral before, curious halfway through." This simple act of recording gives weight to even the smallest shifts. It also makes it easier to notice patterns over time—maybe anything creative lifts your mood a notch, while social activities leave you drained right now.

There's no shame in quitting if something feels wrong or flat. Sometimes a strong "no" is even more valuable than a weak "yes." It means you're paying attention and respecting your limits instead of pushing through out of guilt or habit. One day, painting may bring frustration; another day, it might spark relief or even joy. Both outcomes are valid.

If you need permission, here it is: you're allowed to stop an activity whenever you want. There's no medal for finishing every experiment or forcing yourself into enjoyment that isn't there. The real victory is in showing up for yourself and being honest about what fits and what doesn't.

Sidebar: Permission to quit—sometimes walking away from an activity is not just okay, but important information about where your energy and interest truly belong right now.

The truth is that rediscovering what you like isn't about finding "the thing" that fixes everything. It's about honoring your curiosity, giving yourself choice without pressure, and learning what feels good—or doesn't—one safe experiment at a time.

Celebrating Tiny Victories: Building Self-Trust One Choice at a Time

Every time you make a choice that feels even slightly true to who you are, you're taking a bold step toward reclaiming your sense of self. These steps don't have to be dramatic. In fact, the tiniest victories deserve the loudest cheers. A close friend once told me how she finally decided what to have for breakfast—just toast and jam, nothing fancy. It was the first time in months she'd actually asked herself what she wanted, and the pride she felt was real. She texted a friend, "I made a choice for me today." That simple meal became a small flag planted in the ground—a signal that her voice still mattered, even if it was quiet.

Tracking these micro-wins isn't about bragging or proving anything to anyone else. It's about giving your mind and body evidence that you're capable of making decisions, no matter how minor they seem. One of my favorite practical tools is the "Victory Jar." Find an old jar or small box and keep it somewhere you'll see every day. Each time you notice yourself making a self-affirming choice—saying yes to a walk, choosing your own mug, taking a break when you're tired—write it on a scrap of paper and drop it in the jar. By the end of the week or month, you'll have a visual reminder that you are making progress, even on days when your mind tells you otherwise.

For those who like a visual boost, printable mini-certificates can be surprisingly uplifting. These don't need to be anything formal. A sticky note that says, "I named a preference today!" or "I tried something new without apologizing" can turn an ordinary moment into something you actually see and remember. It's not about reaching perfection; it's about honoring the steps that most people overlook. If paper isn't your thing, try a daily checklist—just a small tick mark for each act of self-assertion, like choosing what music to play or deciding when to rest.

What's happening behind the scenes when you celebrate these victories is actually pretty cool. Every time you recognize a win, your brain releases little bursts of dopamine—the chemical that helps reinforce rewarding behaviors. This isn't just feel-good science talk; it's literally how new habits and self-trust are formed. Your nervous system starts to associate small acts of self-connection with safety and pride, not with anxiety or fear. Think of it as rewiring yourself for resilience, one choice at a time. Over weeks and months, these little celebrations build up a foundation of confidence. They make it easier to trust yourself next time, which is exactly what trauma tries to take away.

Sharing these wins with someone you trust can make them even more powerful. If you have a friend, therapist, or supportive online group, consider sending a quick message or posting about your micro-wins. "I picked out my own lunch today!" "I turned down an invitation because I needed rest." Not only do you get encouragement from others, but hearing your achievement echoed back to you can make it feel more real. Some people use sticker charts on their fridge or inside their journal—a gold star for every act of self-respect. It might sound silly at first, but these playful touches can bring lightness to the hard work of healing.

Sidebar: No win is too small—each step forward is a radical act of reclaiming your selfhood. Even if all you did today was ask yourself what you wanted for dinner and listen for an answer, that matters. If you took two minutes to notice how your body felt after a walk, that's worth writing down. If you gave yourself permission to leave an event early or say "I'm tired" out loud, celebrate that too.

Building this habit isn't always easy. Old narratives might pop up—voices telling you that tiny efforts are pointless or that bigger changes are needed before you deserve recognition. Those voices are echoes from times when your needs were minimized or dismissed. Each time you acknowledge a micro-win, you're slowly shifting those beliefs and making room for new patterns.

Over time, this collection of tiny victories tells a different story than trauma ever could. You see proof—on paper, in jars, on charts—that you can choose for yourself, again and again. This steady practice lays down new tracks in your brain and heart, making it possible to trust yourself in bigger situations down the line.

Remember this: self-trust isn't built in leaps; it grows through hundreds of small choices made day after day. Celebrate each one—you're building more than just confidence; you're rebuilding the foundation for your authentic self to stand on solid ground. In the next chapter, we'll turn our attention outward and explore how reconnecting with your body can deepen these shifts and bring even more clarity to who you are becoming.

There was a time in my healing journey when everything felt unbearably heavy. In those moments, I turned to prayer and quiet reflection, and the journal and Bible opened in front of me. I found myself asking God what I truly needed, admitting how exhausted I was from trying to solve everything on my own. As I sat in the stillness, a gentle thought emerged: "Focus on the things that bring you joy—let your heart heal in that space." That realization struck me deeply. I suddenly became aware of how much of my time was spent doing things out of obligation, not out of genuine desire. I was keeping company with people who drained me, pursuing projects that didn't fulfill me, and even eating foods I didn't actually enjoy. The disconnect between my choices and my true self became clear. From that day forward, I made a conscious decision to seek out and embrace what genuinely delighted me. I prayed for guidance, asking God to reveal what would truly nourish and soothe my spirit along my healing path.

Make a difference with your review.

Unlock the Power of Sharing

Would you help someone like yourself—someone who's curious about faith, identity, and healing, but maybe a little unsure of where to begin or how to make sense of things?

Most people find new books because of thoughtful reviews. That's why I'm reaching out to you to lend a hand to another seeker of identity and healing, by leaving a review.

To make a difference, simply scan the QR code below and leave a review:

Leave Review

https://bethanyelle.com/ri

If you love the idea of helping others find their way, then we're kindred spirits. Thank you from the bottom of my heart.

Warmly, Bethany Elle

6. Healing the Mind-Body Disconnect

Grounding 101: Simple Practices for Everyday Overwhelm

If you've ever found yourself spaced out in a meeting, forgetting where you put your keys, or feeling like your mind and body aren't working together, you're not alone. For many, especially trauma survivors, this isn't random—it's a coping mechanism when stress or memories take over. Grounding is how you bring yourself back to the present, reconnecting to your body and environment when things get overwhelming.

Grounding isn't mystical or complex. At its essence, grounding uses your senses, movement, or focused attention to anchor you in the now. It acts as a reset when anxiety spikes, emotions surge, or you feel numb and detached. By interrupting dissociation, grounding helps prevent you from mentally spiraling. You don't need anything special—just the willingness to pause and notice your body and surroundings. The simple act of tuning in can stabilize you, even on tough days.

A practical favorite, as previously mentioned, is the 5-4-3-2-1 senses countdown because it's quick, portable, and effective. Here's how it works: Name five things you can see—colors, shapes, anything. Notice four things you can feel—the texture of your clothes, the air, the chair, and your feet on the floor. Listen for three sounds—traffic, birds, the refrigerator's hum. Identify two things you can smell—coffee, a candle, or just the air. Finally, notice one thing you can taste—mint from toothpaste or water. If one sense is tricky, spend a little longer on another. The goal isn't perfection, but presence.

Another grounding method uses temperature and touch. Splashing cold water on your face or holding an ice cube quickly brings you back to the present. The gentle shock grabs your attention and interrupts autopilot. Or, hold any object—a pen, stone, or keys—and focus on every detail: size, weight, color, texture, temperature. Describe it as if someone's never seen it before.

Physical grounding works too: press your feet into the floor and feel the support beneath you. Wiggle your toes, press down through your heels, or—if you're able—stand and feel gravity holding you in place. This isn't just about noticing, but reminding yourself that, right now, you are safe enough to be present.

Your Personalized Grounding Toolkit

A personal grounding toolkit means having options for any setting. At home, keep a basket with a smooth stone, scented lotion, or fidget toy. At work, maybe it's a small object in your pocket or a list of grounding scents like lavender oil in your bag. In public spaces, try subtle techniques: silently name what you see, press your feet to the floor under a table, or trace a coin's edge.

Here's a sample grounding script: "Notice your feet right now. Feel the ground solid beneath them. Notice how your back rests against the chair or your hands touch each other. Name three things that make this space real to you." Adjust these words to fit you—what matters is guiding your mind to something concrete.

Make a list of grounding items and practices—a "grounding

menu"—and keep it where you can easily access it or on your phone. When stress or dissociation takes over, use this menu. Over time, grounding becomes second nature—a signal to your nervous system that you're back in control.

Grounding isn't about ignoring pain or pretending everything's fine. It's about returning to yourself so you can meet life more steadily. Even when the world is overwhelming or memories threaten to pull you away, grounding anchors you in the here and now—real, present, and alive.

Sensing Safety: Using the Body as a Resource

Your body has its own language, often communicating before you find the words. After trauma, those signals can get scrambled: what once meant "safe" might now trigger alarms. Your body may react as if you're in danger even when you aren't. This isn't a weakness—it's your nervous system trying to protect you. Relearning your body's cues is like reconnecting with an old friend after hardship.

Physiological signs of safety are usually subtle. Notice a loosening jaw, a sigh, or a relaxed chest after a hug. When you feel safe, your breath deepens, muscles relax, and your belly softens. When your brain senses threat—even if it's not real—your heart may race, your shoulders tense, you may sweat, or your stomach may tighten. Trauma can blur these signals, so your body may sound the alarm for "false positives"—loud noises, certain smells, or even unfamiliar kindness.

Interoception helps here: it means noticing what's happening inside you—noticing raw sensations, not thoughts or stories. Are you warm or cold? Is your stomach fluttery or calm? Is your chest heavy?

Interoception helps distinguish between real danger and echoes from the past. This is a skill that takes some relearning. Don't worry if it's tricky at first; your body is figuring out which signals are current and which are old.

A slow body scan is a good starting point. Find a comfortable place to sit or lie down. Start at your head and work your way down—notice your forehead, jaw, neck, shoulders, arms, belly, legs, and feet. Where do you feel tension or neutrality? Where do you feel nothing? Numbness is also information: it shows your body is still protecting you. You don't need to "fix" anything—just observe. Ask, "Where do I feel most at ease right now?" It could be your hands, behind your knees, or maybe nowhere today. That's all valid.

Think of moments during your day when you feel the safest—under a warm blanket, in the shower, listening to music, holding a pet. When do you feel most on guard? Maybe at work, around certain people, or in crowds. Noticing these patterns helps you understand what feels comforting and what feels threatening, even if no real danger is present.

Anchoring safety in your body can be simple. Placing your hand over your heart or chest offers reassurance and warmth—it's a way to say, "I'm here." Wrapping up in a blanket ("self-swaddling") can provide comfort. Gentle rocking or giving yourself a hug, even if awkward, soothes the nervous system. These are not childish—they're basic human needs for touch and security.

Building small, safe rituals further supports this sense of security. Try starting your mornings with a stretch under the covers, or placing both hands on your chest to breathe slowly. In the evening, settle in with calming scents or soft music to signal "rest time." Create a cozy corner at home with pillows, soft lighting, or familiar objects where you can retreat on hard days. This isn't escaping—it's creating a sensory sanctuary.

Reflection: Mapping Your Safety Patterns

In a notebook, draw two columns: "Safest Moments" and "Least Safe Moments." Write down three times you felt relaxed or present, and three times you felt tense or uneasy in the past week. Next to each, note your environment—what you heard, smelled, who was with you, the time of day. Look for patterns. This isn't about blame; it's simply noticing what helps you and what doesn't.

Your body can become a resource again—it just takes time, practice, and patience. Listening to your body's signals and treating yourself kindly helps rebuild self-trust from within.

Breathwork for Trauma Survivors—Gentle Pathways In

Breathing is one of those things you do all the time without thinking, yet after trauma, even your breath can feel foreign or unreliable. Some days you might notice your chest is tight, your breathing shallow, or you're holding your breath without meaning to. Other times, breathing too deeply can make you dizzy or anxious. It's as if your body doesn't quite trust itself. Breathwork, when approached with care, can help bridge that gap between what your mind knows and what your body feels. Done gently, it can coax your nervous system toward calm and reconnect you with the present.

Not every breathing exercise feels safe for trauma survivors. Some techniques push for deep inhales or holding the breath, but these can trigger panic or flashbacks if your body associates breathlessness with fear. That's why it's important to move slowly, only trying what feels okay, and always having permission to stop or change course. There is no gold star for "doing it right." If something feels off or too intense, it's not a failure—it's valuable feedback from your body.

Gentle breathwork starts with small, accessible practices that respect where you are. The "sigh of relief" breath is a simple one: take a comfortable inhale through your nose—not too deep—and let the air out slowly through your mouth with an audible sigh. Imagine the sound of relief after a long day. This exhale signals to your nervous system that it can let go, even just a bit. Another option is "counting breaths." Breathe in through your nose for a count of four, then exhale through your mouth for a count of six. The slightly longer out-breath helps shift your body toward relaxation, as exhaling more slowly soothes the stress response.

For many, placing a hand on the belly can guide breath downward, inviting the diaphragm to move and softening tension. Rest your palm just below your ribs and notice the gentle rise and fall. You don't have to force anything. If your breath stays shallow, that's okay—just notice what happens under your hand. Some days you'll feel more movement; other days, less.

Sometimes breathwork brings up discomfort—maybe you get lightheaded or your heart races. That's common and not a sign to push through. If you feel dizzy or uneasy, pause right away. Open your eyes if they were closed, look around the room, or focus on an object to ground yourself. You might prefer to keep your eyes open from the start or do breathwork sitting up instead of lying down. If even gentle breathing feels too much, try humming softly or making a gentle sound on the out-breath. For some, just listening to their breath—without changing it—feels safest. There's no pressure to "fix" anything.

Integrating micro-breathwork into daily life can be surprisingly helpful. You don't need to carve out special time or sit on a yoga mat for benefits. Try one slow breath before a meeting or phone call—a pause that tells your system it's not in danger. At stoplights, while waiting in line, or before answering an email, take three slow breaths, letting the exhale last as long as feels natural. These mini-moments add up; they give your mind and body a chance to connect without overwhelm.

You might find that certain times of day work better for you—maybe in the car before work, in the bathroom if things get tense, or as you lay down at night. Breathwork isn't about transforming every moment into tranquility; it's about giving yourself permission to return to yourself in the smallest ways possible, even for just a few seconds at a time. Over time, these pockets of calm can gently widen the window of what feels safe and possible in your own body.

Creating a "Safe Container" for Big Emotions

Big emotions—anger, panic, shame, grief—can arrive suddenly or build over time, sometimes overwhelming you when least expected. In these moments, it often feels urgent to process or fix these feelings immediately, but that pressure isn't necessary. The "container exercise," adapted from trauma therapy, allows you to temporarily set aside intense emotions, storing them in a mental or physical "container" until you're ready to revisit them. This practice gently reassures your mind and body: you're not ignoring your emotions, just taking a pause until you have the resources to engage with them.

Begin with visualization. Imagine a secure space: a locked box, sturdy chest, safe, or even an entire room with thick walls—choose an image that feels protective and strong to you. It could be a treasure chest with iron bands, a simple metal box, or a peaceful, tucked-away spot. Customize it with details—color, lining, location, a special lock or combination—so it feels personal and effective. If visualizing isn't easy, consider drawing your container, shaping it from clay, or describing it in writing. Specificity helps anchor the idea in your mind.

When emotions surge—a racing heart before a tense conversation, painful memories surfacing in daily life—pause and imagine placing those feelings into your container. Closing your eyes might help you visualize gently setting the emotion or memory inside. Quietly remind yourself: "I'm putting this feeling in my container for now. I'll revisit it when I feel more stable." This isn't denying or suppressing your feelings; it's creating space and maintaining control over when you process them.

Use your container whenever emotions threaten to overwhelm—during anxiety spikes, stressful work moments, painful family dynamics, or intrusive memories. Some people keep a physical object, like a small box or pouch, as a tangible reminder of their container. Holding or seeing this object can reinforce your ability to set aside what is too much in the moment.

There's no restriction on how often you use this tool. In fact, repeated use strengthens the skill. You might revisit your container multiple times a day or address the same emotion many times before you're ready to open it again. This isn't avoidance; it's wise self-protection and pacing. Each time you use your container, you're practicing self-care, building emotional regulation, and affirming trust in your capacity to manage big feelings on your own timeline.

One person I worked with visualized locking away anxiety about a difficult coworker every morning before heading to work, promising themselves they'd revisit those feelings in a safer, quieter space at home. Another relied on their container during family dinners, where old wounds surfaced, using it as a mental life raft during difficult conversations.

Sidebar: Your Container Can Evolve

Your container isn't fixed. As you grow and heal, let it evolve—change its color, size, location, or form to reflect your increasing sense of safety and confidence. Add comforting features: a soft interior, a soundproof door, symbols of resilience, or even a window to let in light. Flexibility is key; let your container change as your needs and self-awareness develop.

You don't have to share your container with anyone unless it makes you feel safer or more supported. Over time, this exercise can shift your relationship with intense feelings: they become manageable visitors, not threats, and you decide when to welcome them back.

Moving Again: Restorative, Non-Threatening Movement Practices

When trauma has touched your life, the body often feels like a battleground. Movement, which once felt natural or even joyful, can suddenly seem risky or foreign. There's no shame in that. You might worry that you'll lose control if you start moving, that uncomfortable memories will come back, or that someone will notice and judge. Sometimes body shame keeps you from trying at all. Even the idea of stretching might sound exhausting, especially if certain positions bring up discomfort or remind you of old pain. All these reactions are common. It's not laziness or weakness; it's your system keeping you safe after what you've been through.

Yet there's another side to this story. Gentle movement can help mend the rift between mind and body. It's not about burning calories or pushing limits. Instead, it's about finding a sense of "okayness" in your own skin, even for a moment. Tiny motions—rolling your shoulders, stretching your arms overhead, turning your head slowly side to side—can signal to your nervous system that it's safe to inhabit your body again. Seated stretching is a simple place to begin if standing feels too vulnerable. Sit in a sturdy chair, plant your feet on the floor, and gently stretch one arm across your chest, then switch sides. Notice the sensation; maybe it feels tight, maybe a little freeing.

Another option is walking meditation. This isn't a mystical practice—just an invitation to notice each step as it happens. Focus on the feel of your heel meeting the ground, the shift of weight through your foot, and the gentle roll forward onto your toes. You can do this at home, in your yard, or down a hallway. Every step is an act of attention—a way of checking in with your body without needing to fix anything.

Guided "shaking off" is another restorative movement that might feel silly at first but can be surprisingly effective. Stand with feet hip-width apart (or sit if standing isn't accessible), and start by gently shaking out your hands. Let the movement travel up your arms and then down into your legs, bouncing softly on your heels if you like. Imagine you're shaking off tension, stress, or even old energy you don't need anymore. There's no right or wrong way to do this—just let your body lead and see what feels tolerable.

A central part of reconnecting with movement is paying attention to whether your body wants to move or rest. This isn't about pushing through discomfort; it's about asking, "Is this a yes or a no for me right now?" If the answer is no, that's perfectly fine—resting is also a form of self-care. You might say to yourself, "Notice if your body wants to move or rest—both are valid." This simple question honors your internal cues and gives you permission to listen instead of forcing.

Building your own movement rituals can turn these moments into anchors throughout the day. Maybe you stretch for two minutes each morning before you even leave bed, rolling ankles and wrists or reaching overhead as far as feels good. Some people love a "dance it out" playlist—a few favorite songs that let them move however they want when emotions build up. Others create an end-of-day routine: gentle neck rolls, shoulder shrugs, or stretching in bed to release tension from work or parenting stress.

None of this needs to look pretty or athletic. The goal isn't performance but reconnection—showing up for yourself in small ways, even when it feels awkward or slow. Over time, these tiny movements add up, helping rebuild trust between mind and body and making space for both ease and energy.

Remember this: feeling at home in your body doesn't happen overnight. Every attempt—whether it's a stretch, a walk around the block, or simply lying still and breathing—is a win. The next chapter will explore self-compassion and how kindness toward yourself can support all these physical practices, deepening both healing and self-trust as you move forward.

One of the grounding practices I rely on most when I need to feel safe is simply walking. The steady rhythm of my footsteps against the earth creates a sense of stability beneath me, helping me return to the present moment. Whether I'm surrounded by the calming embrace of nature or the familiar rhythms of the city, walking soothes my aching heart. It becomes a gentle space for me to process my thoughts, connect with God in prayer, reflect on my next steps, or simply allow myself to just be.

7. Compassion For Self and Reparenting

Meeting Your Inner Child: A Guided Visualization

There's a unique ache that doesn't show in any test or scan but still lives within us—an emptiness or longing, sometimes just a question: "Who's taking care of me now?" Childhood wounds don't just fade with age; they affect how we see ourselves, trust others, and navigate life. Achievements and efforts to "move on" may not satisfy the younger part inside that still yearns for comfort or kindness. This is your inner child—a living memory, the younger self whose hopes, fears, and unmet needs linger and who also carries your potential for healing.

Your inner child isn't an abstract idea but a collection of real memories and needs residing within, especially when life is challenging or old patterns re-emerge. Picture your younger self: the one discovering delight and disappointment for the first time, crumpling under harsh words or glowing from simple joys. For adults who've survived trauma, this inner child may feel hidden or even judged as "too needy." Reconnecting isn't about staying stuck in the past, but about finally offering yourself what was missing. With compassion, you can bridge then and now, rewriting old scripts with the care you needed all along ([23], [31]).

Let's try a gentle visualization. Find a comfortable space where you won't be disturbed. Close your eyes, or soften your gaze, and take a slow, deep breath. Now, recall yourself as a child. Maybe you see yourself at a certain age, or maybe there's just a feeling—a sense of your younger self. Imagine this child in a setting that feels secure, like a sunlit backyard, a cozy fort, or a favorite chair. Notice details: age, clothing, posture—are they tense, relaxed, guarded, curious? Let the image or feeling surface naturally.

Notice your inner child's expression. Do they show worries, playfulness, or sadness? Approach with curiosity. Silently ask: "What does this child need to feel safe right now?" Perhaps it's a hug, kind words, a listener, or just space to play free of adult concerns. You may get images or feelings, or even a sense in your body; trust whatever surfaces.

If this visualization feels challenging, that's okay—especially if early trust was broken. Your mind may go blank or the picture may fade. This is normal. Try drawing your inner child—stick figures or simple colors are enough. Or write a letter to them, letting the words flow without judging or overthinking. If nothing comes, remember: this is practice, not a test. Your efforts count.

Bringing your inner child into daily life creates an ongoing relationship—don't visit just when in crisis. Set a daily reminder to "Check in with my inner child." Make a bedtime ritual: mentally tuck your inner child in at the end of each day. Place an old photo nearby or keep a soft object—like a blanket, stone, or stuffed animal—as a discreet comfort. These small gestures anchor you to that younger self, saying, "I see you."

Interactive Element: Reflection Prompt

After practicing the visualization, drawing, or writing, reflect in your journal:

- What did I notice about my inner child's emotions or body language?
- What did they seem to need from me today?
- How did it feel to offer comfort—awkward, sad, relieving, or something else?

Return to these questions whenever you want to strengthen this connection. Each small act of caring rewrites the belief that you're alone with your needs.

Connecting with your inner child isn't about self-blame for the past but about showing up now as the steady, caring adult you always deserved. Even just recognizing your inner child is enough to begin. Healing starts with simple acknowledgment and the commitment not to ignore those brave, sensitive parts of yourself ever again.

Scripts for Self-Soothing During Setbacks

Setbacks hit hard—sometimes out of nowhere, sometimes after a slow build of stress and overwhelm. You might feel your chest tighten, thoughts start to spiral, or that heavy wave of self-criticism roll in. In those moments, it's easy to forget every tool and bit of wisdom you've picked up, so having ready-made words to lean on can make all the difference. Consider these scripts as emotional first-aid, simple phrases you can whisper or say aloud when things get rough: "It's okay to feel this way. I'm here for you." Or, "This is hard, but it's not forever. I can take care of myself right now." These aren't about fixing what hurts in an instant—they're about letting yourself know you aren't alone with your pain.

You don't have to stick to these scripts exactly. The beauty is in making them yours. For anxiety, you might say, "Right now, I feel scared. I can breathe slowly and remind myself I'm safe." If shame creeps in, try: "I did the best I could with what I knew. I am not my mistakes." When anger bubbles up, a gentle reminder could be, "I notice my anger. It makes sense after what I've been through. I can let it move through me safely." Sadness might ask for a softer touch: "This feeling is heavy, but it will pass. I deserve patience and comfort." You can even jot down your own phrases—sometimes the words that come most naturally are the ones that soothe the deepest.

Pairing words with physical comfort can multiply their power. Place a hand over your heart or wrap your arms around yourself in a light hug. Notice how warmth or gentle pressure shifts something inside. If it's available, wrap up in a favorite blanket or pull on a cozy sweater—textures matter, especially when the world feels sharp or cold. Rocking gently in a chair or side to side while repeating soothing words can signal safety to your nervous system. Try adding a calming scent—lavender oil dabbed on your wrist, a favorite candle burning nearby, or even the smell of fresh laundry. While you offer these comforts, speak your chosen script out loud or silently. The combination of words and physical touch anchors you in the present and reminds both body and mind that care is possible.

The real magic comes from practicing these scripts and actions when things are calm—not just during storms. Rehearse in front of a mirror on a neutral day, just to get used to the sound and shape of the words in your mouth. Record yourself saying your script on your phone and play it back before sleep or first thing in the morning. The more familiar these words become, the easier it is to reach for them when distress smacks you out of nowhere. Sticky notes help too—put them on your bathroom mirror, fridge, or inside your planner. Seeing a reminder like "I am safe now" or "I deserve kindness" at random moments can work quietly in the background, building new pathways in your mind.

Scripts aren't magic that banish pain, but they do create small openings for relief and self-compassion in tough times. You might fumble with the words at first or feel silly talking to yourself out loud—this is normal. Every time you practice, you're building a bridge back to yourself, one phrase at a time. Over weeks and months, these new scripts become part of your automatic self-talk, slowly shifting how you relate to setbacks and emotions. If you ever feel stuck on what to say, remember: gentleness is enough. Even a simple "It's okay to be struggling right now" can interrupt old patterns of shame and replace them with something softer and true.

Permission to Go Slow: Redefining "Progress"

Somewhere along the way, this idea got planted in us—that healing should look spectacular, or at least move at a steady, upward pace. The truth for most trauma survivors is so much messier and, honestly, more human. Progress isn't a highlight reel or a dramatic breakthrough. Sometimes it's the tiniest shift: catching yourself before snapping at someone, pausing to take one deep breath before reacting, or simply noticing that the shame voice isn't quite as loud as yesterday. There are days when the biggest victory is opting to rest instead of beating yourself up for not being productive. These moments often slip by unnoticed because they don't fit the story we've been told about what "real" healing looks like. But they matter.

I've witnessed people measure their worth by how quickly they can "bounce back," and end up feeling worse when life refuses to cooperate. The truth is, slow steps are not lesser steps. Pausing before you react—even if you still get overwhelmed—is progress. Feeling a bit less bothered by something that used to crush you? That's huge. Deciding to eat lunch instead of skipping it as punishment for a bad morning? That's growth. These micro-movements may not impress anyone else, but inside, they're proof that your nervous system, your heart, your whole self is learning something new.

If you want to make these shifts real and visible to yourself, try keeping a "Noticing Moments of Gentleness" log. Grab a notebook or open a new note on your phone. Jot down small moments—no matter how small—where you offered yourself a sliver of kindness. Maybe you whispered, "That's enough for today," or allowed yourself an hour of mindless TV without guilt. You might write: "Today I gave myself a break when I felt tired at work and didn't force myself to keep going." Or: "I paused and noticed the sun on my face before going back inside." These logs aren't about finding things to brag about; they're about building evidence that you're changing from the inside out, one gentle choice at a time.

You set your own pace in this work. Some days you'll have energy for reflection or practice; other days, just making it through is enough. Healing doesn't care about calendars or other people's expectations. Your needs and capacity will fluctuate—sometimes wildly. Remember, it helps to visualize growth not as a straight line but as something organic. Imagine growth rings in a tree trunk—some years wide with expansion, others narrow and tough, but always adding up over time. Or picture a spiral that loops back on itself, yet keeps widening outwards with each pass. Progress might mean cycling back to earlier chapters or pausing entirely for a week or more. That's not failure; it's honoring your own rhythm.

My friend, Jenna, said, "Every time I thought I was stuck, I was actually learning something new about myself." She stopped comparing her pace to anyone else's and started celebrating each insight as it came—sometimes days apart, sometimes months.

Taking breaks is part of healing—not a detour or a mistake. If you need to reread a chapter three times or walk away from these practices for a while, that's allowed. Sometimes the most healing thing you can do is nothing at all. Try scheduling intentional "healing rest days" where your only goal is to be gentle with yourself—no pressure for insight or change. Put your hand on your heart and say, "Today, I'm resting." Notice how even this act can feel radical.

Visual: Growth Rings Metaphor

Imagine your progress as concentric rings of a tree—each layer representing another year or season of quiet effort. Some rings are thin and close together, marking tough periods; others are wider and brighter, showing times when change felt easier or more obvious. Over time, all those rings add up to something strong and sturdy, even if growth was invisible to the outside world.

Healing isn't a race—pauses and slow spells are part of the path. Every gentle choice, every skipped self-criticism, every moment you let yourself just be is a win worth noticing and honoring.

Forgiving Yourself for Not Healing Faster

The pressure to heal quickly can often feel more burdensome than the pain itself. Many of us carry a quiet self-blame, believing we "should be further along" or that others seem to recover so much faster. Perhaps you were raised to quickly move on from pain or have seen polished "before and after" stories online that gloss over the hard, slow work of real recovery. These expectations take hold early and are hard to shake, making it easy to judge your own worth by comparing yourself to others' timelines or to social media highlight reels. You may wonder why your pain persists or why setbacks keep occurring, even long after the worst has passed. It's normal to feel both frustrated and worried that you're somehow failing at recovery.

This frustration is often rooted in comparison. You catch yourself looking at how friends, family, or even strangers seem to heal seamlessly, making you want to rush your own process. It's not always about others; sometimes it's that internal voice repeating things you once heard from a parent or teacher: "Aren't you over this yet?" But trauma doesn't follow schedules—healing depends on your nervous system and sense of safety. Some wounds heal quickly; others take time. There's no right speed.

If you're stuck between wanting to move on and feeling ashamed for not being "there" yet, pause. Place your hand over your heart or cheek for comfort. As odd as it may seem, gently say: "I forgive myself for believing I should be further along. My pace is my own." Notice any doubt or resistance, and let it be without forcing it away. Imagine the part of you that feels left behind—whether it's a shadow, a tired version of yourself, or a heavy feeling. Send it warmth and kindness, as if wrapping it in a soft blanket or lighting it gently. Sometimes these neglected parts just need to feel acknowledged.

Simple affirmations can help when you sense that old pressure to move faster: “It’s okay to be exactly where I am.” Or, “Progress is not measured by speed, but by presence and courage.” Echo these words when impatience or comparison flares—when you envy others’ paths or wish your own were easier. You might write these affirmations on sticky notes or repeat them in the shower. The point isn’t to erase impatience, but to remind yourself that simply showing up matters more than racing ahead.

There are many ways people learn to honor their own pace. For example, someone once told me they set aside their journal for an entire year after feeling burned out on self-work. When they returned to it a year later, they found fresh insights waiting—they hadn’t lost anything by waiting. Another survivor shared, "It took me ten years to feel ready for therapy after a bad experience, and that’s okay." Stories like these are reminders that healing can pause and restart many times, and each attempt is an act of courage, whenever it occurs.

If old stories about “falling behind” start up again, try writing a letter to your future self—one who moved at their own pace and still found healing. Or picture a gathering of people with timelines that don’t fit the mold, standing in solidarity instead of shame. Everyone heals differently; every step, no matter the speed or visibility, deserves respect. Your process is enough—even if it feels slow or unseen.

Affirmations and Self-Compassion Practices for Daily Life

After trauma, your mind can seem like it’s working against you, replaying judgments and doubts on repeat. This isn't just a habit—it's how trauma changes your brain, reinforcing harsh self-talk. The good news is your brain is adaptable. As I mentioned earlier, neuroplasticity can lay down new pathways and create gentle, supportive thoughts where old criticism lingered ([26]). Affirmations help with this—not as magic, but as a consistent, caring practice. They offer your mind a new language, shifting your self-talk from blame toward compassion. With practice, these phrases loosen the tight hold of shame and fear.

The key to trauma-sensitive affirmations is credibility. If "I love myself" feels out of reach, start softer: "I am learning to be kind to myself," or "It's safe to grow at my own pace." The important thing is that your words feel honest and offer even a small sense of possibility. Examples include: "I am worthy of kindness, especially from myself," "All of my feelings are welcome," "Today, I choose patience with myself," and "It's okay to rest." Adjust the words so they fit your voice—maybe "I'm doing my best right now," or "Small steps count." Substitute language that suits your beliefs or culture. What matters is honesty and warmth, not perfection.

For affirmations to work, they should fit seamlessly into your daily life. There's no need for a dedicated affirmation session. Write one on your bathroom mirror with a dry-erase marker so it's visible each morning. Put a kind phrase on a sticky note in your wallet or lunchbox. Make an affirmation your phone background for regular exposure. Tie a phrase to a daily habit—say it while brushing your teeth or making coffee. These routines become gentle reminders throughout the day, helping to guide your self-talk naturally.

Affirmations can also serve as resets in stressful moments. After a difficult conversation or meeting, pause to breathe and repeat: "I can handle this; I am safe now." When shame or anxiety returns after a mistake, remind yourself: "Everyone stumbles. I am allowed to learn and move forward." These phrases are like a gentle hand on your shoulder, supporting you during tough times.

A compassion ritual doesn't need to be complex. Try a quick five-minute check-in before bed or after waking—close your eyes and ask, "How am I feeling?" Ask God what you need in that moment. Write your answer without judging it. Or start a compassion jar: every time you show self-kindness—even in small ways, like speaking gently to yourself or taking a break—note it on a slip of paper and add it to the jar. Over time, these notes become visible proof of your progress and growth in self-kindness.

If you find motivation in connection, choose an affirmation each week to text to a friend who's practicing compassion too, or share it in a supportive online group. Speaking affirmations out loud, especially with someone supportive, can give them even greater meaning and power.

Self-compassion doesn't mean you'll never struggle or that self-love comes easily. It's about changing your inner dialogue so that, when you're hurting, your first impulse is understanding rather than shame. Affirmations are daily acts of protest against your old patterns, reminders that healing is possible and that you matter enough to care for.

Remember this: affirmations and compassion rituals are not quick fixes, but steady tools to gently rewire how you treat yourself from within. Each attempt counts, even if it feels clumsy or slow. In the next chapter, you'll learn to move from inner work toward creating safe, supportive boundaries with others—carrying your growing self-compassion into your relationships and daily life.

The Bible teaches us, "Love your neighbor as yourself," reminding us that self-love and compassion are foundational to how we care for others. Yet, in many Christian circles, we're often encouraged to focus solely on loving others, neglecting the equally important practice of loving ourselves. Through my own healing journey, I realized that I could not truly extend the love and kindness God calls us to if I was not first gentle and compassionate with myself. Embracing self-care and self-acceptance became not just a necessary step for my own healing, but a powerful way to authentically love those around me.

8. Boundary-Building Blueprints

What a Boundary Really Is (and Isn't)

Ever felt drained after a late-night call where you're expected to listen endlessly, or when a coworker piles tasks onto you simply because you always say yes? The exhaustion or resentment that follows stems from a lack of boundaries—not thick walls, but invisible lines that signal, "This is where I end and you begin." Boundaries aren't selfish or rude—they're a way to protect your well-being while still respecting others.

Myths abound: Some people believe boundaries mean cutting loved ones off or acting cold, or assume only the "difficult" need them. In fact, setting limits is a mark of self-respect and maturity—especially vital after trauma, which can blur your sense of self. Boundaries aren't punishments. They're guidelines for what feels safe and respectful to you, much like property lines around a house. These lines have doors and windows—allowing connection, not keeping everyone out.

Trauma can scramble boundaries. If you were hurt or ignored, you may lose track of your limits. Some grow up thinking "good people" never say no, or have their comfort repeatedly steamrolled until their boundaries vanish. Others respond by erecting high walls and disconnecting from everyone. Still others have such porous boundaries that they absorb everyone else's stress, desires, and problems—leaving them drained and lost.

There are three main types of boundaries: healthy, rigid, and porous. Healthy boundaries are like adjustable fences—flexible, opening for the right people, closing when you need rest or privacy. Rigid boundaries are more like fortress walls; little comes in or out, so you might be safe from harm but miss intimacy. Porous boundaries are like gardens without fences; everyone's issues become yours, and your energy is sapped.

For trauma survivors reclaiming their identities, boundaries are essential. They aren't just about saying no, but about rediscovering what matters to you and safeguarding it. Without boundaries, it's easy to shape-shift into whatever those around you want, losing sight of your own needs and values. This feeds resentment and burnout. Boundaries help you see where your responsibilities end and another's begin, creating space for your preferences and values—key pieces of self that trauma often muddies.

Visualize your boundary as an invisible fence for your spirit—not keeping others out, but helping you spot when someone's crowding you or when you're giving too much. These fences can adapt as you grow. Maybe now you need more space; later, you might safely let people closer.

Reflection: Mapping Your Boundary Spectrum

Take a notebook and draw a line labeled "Porous" at one end, "Rigid" at the other, and "Healthy" in the middle. Consider different parts of your life—work, family, friends, relationships, online communities—and mark where your boundaries currently fall along that line. Do some areas feel too loose, some too tight? You may be lenient with family but strict at work. This isn't about judgment; it's just a snapshot.

Ask yourself:

- Where do I feel most drained or resentful?
- When do I leave conversations feeling small or invisible?
- Do I say yes when I mean no?
- Who makes me uncomfortable with physical affection or demands?

Notice any patterns: maybe you're always the emotional support for friends but shut down at home. Maybe certain topics (like money or health) leave you frozen or too accommodating. This isn't about blame—it's about seeing where you could reinforce or adjust your "fence."

Boundaries aren't just about saying no; they're about saying yes to yourself. This might mean carving out quiet time after work instead of replying to every message right away, or limiting how much family drama you allow into your day. Maybe it means hugs are for safe people only, or not discussing certain topics with certain relatives.

Building and maintaining boundaries is ongoing—there's no perfect balance. Some days you'll hold firm; other times you'll revert to old habits. That's normal. Over time, as you tune in to what feels best for you, boundary-setting becomes more intuitive and easier. Each effort reclaims another part of yourself from the effects of trauma.

If you're not sure where your boundaries might be thin, use this quick checklist:

- Do I feel guilty when taking time for myself?
- Is it hard to say no without a lengthy explanation?
- Do I often feel resentful after helping others?
- Do I allow unwanted physical touch?
- Have I agreed to things to avoid conflict?
- Do I share more than feels comfortable?
- Is my energy mainly spent managing others' feelings?

See which questions make you pause or feel discomfort. This isn't a test—it's a chance to gently notice which areas could benefit from small changes for your well-being.

Boundaries aren't about shutting out love—they're invitations for mutual respect. They show you (and the world) how you want to be treated, and help you remember what matters most (see source 1).

Scripts for Saying "No" Without Apology

Saying "no" often feels daunting, especially if your past taught you to put your needs last or avoid conflict. Trauma can create a belief that saying "no" leads to trouble, rejection, or even danger. However, rebuilding your sense of self means learning that "no" isn't just safe—it's vital. You don't need to justify, apologize for, or shrink yourself to set limits. Sometimes, the most respectful thing you can say is a clear, simple "no."

When learning to refuse, it helps to have clear phrases at hand. You don't need to be clever—directness often works best, minimizing misunderstanding and negotiation. In moments where your instinct says "no" but speaking up is hard, use phrases like: "I'm not able to do that," "That doesn't work for me," or even just "No, thank you." For situations where you want even less explanation: simply say "No." These statements protect your needs without overextending yourself. If directness feels too intense or unsafe, gentle refusals work too: "I appreciate the offer, but I'll pass," or "I need to sit this one out." Non-verbal cues—shaking your head, stepping back, or a small smile with a decline—also signal refusal.

How you deliver your words matters. Body language and tone convey confidence, even if you're nervous. Maintain a relaxed but upright posture. Meet the other person's eyes briefly—just enough to show sincerity, not aggression. Speak at a normal pace and volume; rushing or whispering can undermine your "no." If anxiety makes your voice unsteady, try grounding yourself by pressing your feet into the floor or taking a slow breath before responding. These subtle actions help you remain centered. The aim isn't to sound forceful or robotic—just to let your "no" stand on its own.

Many people get caught over-explaining refusals, especially trauma survivors keen to avoid upset. Offering context is fine if you want, but it's never required. Notice the difference between a straightforward "No, I won't be able to," and a guilt-driven, "I'm so sorry, I have a lot going on, maybe next time…" The first protects your time and energy; the second often invites pushback or guilt. Remember: "No" is a complete sentence. The impulse to justify usually arises from old patterns—not your real needs.

If saying no feels awkward, that's normal. Practice in low-stakes situations can build confidence for harder moments. Write refusals in a journal: "No, I'm not available," "That doesn't fit my schedule," or "I'm choosing not to." Stand in front of the mirror and repeat your lines out loud, paying attention to your tone and posture. You could also try role-playing with a friend who can offer gentle feedback or just listen.

These small rehearsals make real refusals less intimidating over time. Consider moments where you may need to say no: declining a social invitation when you need rest, refusing extra work that isn't yours, setting a limit on requests for money, not answering intrusive family questions, or turning down unwanted physical affection. Write out or imagine your response for each scenario.

When words seem stuck during real conversations, rely on micro-practices: take a slow breath before responding, place a hand over your heart if that calms you, or visualize a small shield between yourself and the other person as you speak. With time, these habits become natural.

Here are five practice scenarios:

1. A friend invites you out after work when you need rest.
2. Your boss asks you to stay late again, even after overtime.
3. A relative broaches an uncomfortable topic at dinner.
4. Someone reaches for a hug, but you'd prefer a handshake.
5. A neighbor asks for help moving heavy furniture on your day off.

Write out or rehearse your "no" for each. Notice which ones feel easy or stir up anxiety or guilt. If some seem impossible right now, that's fine—start with the lowest-risk area and build from there.

The more often you say no without apology or excessive explanation, the more natural it feels to honor your limits in both big and small ways. Each time you stand by your boundaries—without shrinking or explaining—you reclaim a bit more of yourself from whatever past experience tried to erase it.

Navigating Guilt and Pushback from Loved Ones

The first time you set a boundary, guilt often arrives uninvited. You may feel as though you're letting someone down or abandoning your role as the fixer or dependable one. This is a learned response, rooted in experiences where people-pleasing felt safer. Perhaps saying no was discouraged, or approval brought you a sense of belonging. If you're used to prioritizing others, guilt gets entangled with your self-worth. Past trauma can intensify the fear of being punished or abandoned for asserting yourself, making these moments feel almost primal—chest tight, palms sweaty, ground shifting beneath you.

Recognizing that guilt is a conditioned response helps weaken its hold. It doesn't mean you're selfish; it's just old wiring reacting to new behavior. Family and close friends often reinforce this guilt unintentionally. When you assert a limit, even gently, their reactions may surprise you. They can act hurt, question your motives, or bring up all the times you've helped before: "You always used to help me!" or "Why are you being this way?" Some respond with anger, complaints, or even silence—the silent treatment, which sparks anxiety. Others may guilt-trip or suggest you're ungrateful. The more you defend yourself, the more complicated it can become.

Pushback appears in many guises. Some will try to override your boundary with arguments—"You're just tired, you'll change your mind." Others use emotional tactics: sighing, sulking, or crying. A parent might say, "I guess I can't count on you anymore," triggering old insecurities. Friends may joke that you've changed or suggest something's wrong. These reactions can cause your nervous system to go on alert, pushing you to second-guess yourself or back down.

Anticipating pushback makes it less jarring. Prepare simple responses in advance: "I hear this is disappointing," or "I still care about you, but this is something I need." Often, repeating your boundary calmly is more effective than getting drawn into debate. If someone protests—"I don't get why you can't come over like before"—steady yourself and reply: "I know this is hard to hear. I love you, but I need to make this change." Long explanations aren't necessary—clarity and brevity are your allies.

Guilt won't vanish immediately. When it arises, acknowledge it, but don't let it dictate your actions. Affirmations like, "It's okay to disappoint others to honor myself," or "Guilt is a feeling, not a fact. My needs matter," can anchor you. Say them aloud, write them down—small reminders help reinforce your resolve.

When anxiety spikes or old habits tempt you to retreat, grounding techniques are useful. Take a breath. Plant your feet firmly on the floor. Imagine your boundary as a gentle shield—a means to healthy connection, not rejection. Visualize a supportive friend by your side, encouraging you.

Practical strategies help maintain boundaries under pressure. The "broken record" technique is effective: calmly repeat your statement rather than engaging in fresh arguments. If someone insists—"Can't you just make an exception?"—reply with the same phrase: "I'm not able to do that," or "That doesn't work for me right now." Repeat as needed.

Setting time limits for difficult conversations can be helpful. If a discussion grows too heated or circular, say, "I can talk about this for ten more minutes, then I need to step away." This respects both parties and gives you an exit plan if things get overwhelming.

If things escalate or the pressure is too much, excuse yourself before resentment builds: "I need a break—I'll check back in later when we're calmer." Stepping away protects your energy; it's not running from conflict but choosing self-preservation. Time apart lets emotions settle for a more constructive return.

Use positive self-talk: "Upholding boundaries is self-respect, even if others don't see it." Quietly repeat: "My needs are valid even if someone disagrees." If guilt lingers, consider what values you honored—rest, honesty, or self-care—and why they matter to you.

Navigating guilt and pushback takes repeated effort and patience. Some days will be tougher; old patterns fade gradually. Each time you hold a boundary—even if shakily—you reinforce that your needs matter. Over time, loved ones may adjust and respect your limits. If they don't, that reflects their struggle with change, not your worth.

Practicing Boundaries at Work, Home, and with Friends

Boundaries are more than theory—they're shaped and tested in daily life. Maybe you dread your boss's "Can you handle this, too?" email, crave a few peaceful minutes at home after work, only to face family demands, or get a late-night call from a friend who needs to vent when you're exhausted. These moments challenge your limits and provide real practice in protecting your energy.

At work, setting boundaries can feel tricky because of power dynamics, especially if you've faced consequences for speaking up in the past. Still, it's doable. For example, if you're overwhelmed, say, "I'm at capacity right now and can't take on more." This response is clear, honest, and not negotiable. If coworkers expect responses after hours, set a standard: "I handle work emails between 9 and 5. I'll get back to you tomorrow." You're not being difficult—just clear. If your supervisor ignores your limit and adds more tasks, restate your boundary: "I want to do my best work, but my current workload won't allow it." If this keeps happening, consider escalating or documenting your requests. Each time you reinforce your boundary, you strengthen your self-respect.

At home, boundaries often feel more tangled because of deep routines and expectations. Maybe you want thirty minutes alone after work, but family members immediately ask for help. It's okay to say, "I need 30 minutes to myself after work. I'll join you when I'm ready." You're expressing your needs, not rejecting your family. If you're shouldering all the chores or emotional labor, try, "I'd like us to revisit how we split things up. It's too much for me right now." Initial discomfort is normal, especially if you're known for overextending yourself. Be patient and consistent—change takes time.

Kids make boundaries more challenging because they may not understand them yet. Still, modeling boundaries teaches important lessons. If your child interrupts your rest, explain: "I need some quiet time right now. I'll come out when I'm done." Over time, they'll learn that everyone's needs matter, starting with watching you honor your own.

With friends, boundaries mean not always playing therapist or declining invitations that drain you. If a friend relies on you for support without reciprocating, you might say, "I care about you, but don't have the capacity to support you that way right now." When someone brings up a topic you'd rather avoid—gossip, personal details—redirect or say, "I'm not up for talking about that." If you need to turn down an invite, a simple "Thanks for thinking of me, but I'll have to pass this time" suffices—you don't need elaborate excuses.

Some situations escalate quickly. If a manager ignores your boundaries after reminders, keep a record of your communication. If a family member escalates—by getting upset or raising their voice—don't quickly give in or try to fix things. Calmly acknowledge their feelings: "I see this is hard for you," and return to your boundary. If they persist, let them know you're open to talking later, once things are calmer.

Friends may push even after you've said no. It's important to stick to your decision: "I appreciate your invitation, but my answer is still no." Don't feel responsible for managing their disappointment. Calm, consistent repetition is powerful.

You might stumble or have doubts at first. That's normal. Celebrate each time you honor your limit, no matter how small. Try keeping a "boundary wins" log on your phone or in a journal—note moments like "Said no to overtime," "Took five minutes alone after dinner," or "Declined a late-night call." These small victories build confidence over time.

Reward yourself for maintaining boundaries—enjoy a favorite snack, go for a walk, listen to music, or just affirm: "That was hard, and I did it." Sharing these moments with trusted friends or a support group can make boundary-setting feel more normal and gratifying.

One woman shared about telling her sibling she couldn't mediate every family argument anymore. She expected anger but instead felt lighter and more authentic, even if her sibling was upset. That empowered feeling grew and carried into her other relationships.

Boundary-setting is often messy and never perfect. Discomfort fades as the benefits appear—more energy, less resentment, and a clearer sense of self.

Practicing boundaries every day—at work, home, and with friends—improves your relationships and your connection with yourself. These skills aren't just tools to get by; they're the foundation for living on your terms, especially after trauma or challenging times.

Remember this: Every boundary you set, even imperfectly, is a statement that your needs matter. Next, we'll explore how real connection grows when boundaries create space for genuine trust and closeness.

Learning to set healthy boundaries was a challenging journey for me. At times, I found myself swinging between being overly rigid and having no boundaries at all. It was a gradual process, often filled with uncertainty and self-doubt. Throughout this season, I leaned heavily on prayer, seeking guidance for how to protect my well-being while remaining open to others. In my reflections on scripture, I discovered that even God models boundaries—demonstrating their importance in every relationship. Embracing this truth gave me the courage and wisdom to establish boundaries rooted in both self-care and respect, helping me to rebuild authentic, healthy connections with others..

9. Pathways to Authentic Connection

Safe People, Safe Spaces—How to Identify Real Support

Imagine you're at work or a family gathering. The room buzzes with conversation, yet a tightness fills your chest. You scan for someone who brings calm—the sense that, sitting beside them, you could breathe more easily. For trauma survivors, this need for safety in relationships isn't merely comfort—it's about survival. Trauma can jumble your instincts about trust, leaving you second-guessing your feelings, blaming yourself for needing space, or wondering if you're too sensitive. Learning to spot "safe people" and create "safe spaces" is a vital skill, not about finding perfection or isolating yourself, but about honoring what feels supportive.

A safe person respects your boundaries and never pressures you to share or act before you're ready. They listen—truly listen—without interrupting or trying to fix your feelings. Around safe people, you don't feel hurried or judged; there's a steady acceptance, whether you're struggling or silent. They don't demand your story, poke at wounds, or act from curiosity. Their empathy is real—they believe you, validate your pain, and let you set the pace. If you need space, they give it; if you want closeness, it comes without strings. Safe people give space for boundaries or limits.

Emotional safety registers in your body. You may notice your shoulders relax or your breath slow down with someone trustworthy—

no stomach knots, no urge to escape, no need for a mask. You can be messy, tired, uncertain, or joyful without apology. Safe spaces offer similar relief: they protect your privacy, welcome you without pressure, and allow you to leave if discomfort arises. It could be a chair by a window, a cozy nook with blankets, your car with quiet music—anywhere your nervous system unwinds.

Not every person or place is safe, and unsafe ones often stand out more. Relationship red flags include invalidation ("You're overreacting," "That never happened"), gaslighting, pressure to share before you're ready, or someone trying to "fix" you instead of just being there. If someone laughs off your boundaries, dismisses your pain, betrays your confidence, or expects you to carry their emotional weight, these are signs to be cautious.

Safe Connection Checklist

Reflect on these:

Safe Person Audit

- Do they listen without interrupting or giving advice?
- Can you say "no" without guilt or backlash?
- Do they respect your pace, including silence?
- Are they reliable and consistent?
- Have they ever shamed you for how you feel?
- Are their boundaries clear—they share but don't overshare?

Safe Space Audit

- Is your privacy honored—no prying or gossip?
- Can you leave without drama?
- Is the setting predictable and calm?
- Are expectations about topics and timing clear?
- Do you feel physically comfortable—no crowding or chaos?

Your body is often the first to sense whether someone or somewhere feels supportive. Do you relax or tense up around them? Does your chest open or close? Do you lean in or look for escape? These cues are shaped by your history; trauma might scramble intuition, but with attention, you can rebuild trust in your signals.

Recall a recent moment you truly felt safe with someone. Perhaps it was a friend listening without fixing, or a sibling quietly sitting with you. What did your body feel like? What did that person do to make you feel calm?

If safety isn't possible with people nearby, create "pockets of safety" for yourself. Avoid or limit time with draining, unsettling individuals—even short breaks help. Make a "safe corner" at home: a reading nook, porch space, or your bed with calming music. At work, a plant or soothing screensaver can offer a brief retreat. Keep a list—on your phone or notebook—of safe contacts: someone who replies to texts, a therapist's voicemail, a supportive group chat.

Setting boundaries with less-safe people requires practice. Use clear statements: "I'm not comfortable talking about that," "I need time alone," or "Let's change the subject." If you fear directness, keep conversations short or neutral. Protecting your energy isn't selfish—it's an act of survival.

Notice which people and places help you breathe easier and which leave you tense. The more you pay attention, the more confidently you can seek genuine support and carve out havens for healing.

Micro-Connections: Reaching Out When You Feel Like Hiding

After trauma, it's normal to want to retreat; the world can feel harsh and conversations risky, making hiding seem like safety—a shield from judgment and overwhelm. Solitude may bring short-term relief, but prolonged isolation grows heavier, feeding loneliness and eroding confidence in your ability to connect. Even the idea of reaching out can bring panic or shame, especially if you've been disconnected for a while. That's why micro-connections—small, manageable moments of contact—are so valuable. They gently erode isolation without demanding more than you can give.

Consider Jamie, who spent months speaking to almost no one outside of work. Friends' invitations felt burdensome. She craved connection but felt exposed and unable to remember how to converse normally. One rough night, she sent a simple thumbs-up emoji to a friend. The friend responded with a heart. It didn't solve everything, but it made Jamie feel less invisible. Gradually, she started to reach out more—short texts, comments, small social gestures. Those micro-steps slowly rebuilt her confidence and softened her loneliness.

Micro-connections are like social stretching. Instead of diving into long conversations or big gatherings, take a small risk—a text, a wave, a short hello. These don't require deep talk or emotional effort; they simply remind you that connection is possible and safe enough to attempt again tomorrow. Sending a smiley face, liking a photo, nodding at a neighbor, or making eye contact with the cashier—each counts. Even when you're low on words or energy, these simple gestures prepare the ground for bigger connections.

On low-energy days, reach for the easiest options: react to a story with an emoji, give a quick thumbs-up. If you have a bit more energy, comment "lol" on a meme or tag someone in a funny post. For some, asynchronous contact—texts or emails—feels safest because you don't need to reply right away. On higher-energy days, send a "thinking of you" text or share a cheerful article. When you're up for a slightly bigger effort, try a five-minute phone call or briefly drop by an event, knowing you can leave early if needed.

Connection isn't limited to words or screens. Mail a postcard with just "Hi! Hope you're ok." Leave a sticky note for your roommate: "Thanks for the coffee." Send a meme to your sibling. These tiny acts create ripples of connection that don't exhaust your reserves.

If you haven't talked to someone in ages and it feels awkward, try low-pressure messages like: "No need to respond, just wanted you to know I'm thinking of you," or "It's been a while, but you crossed my mind and I hope you're well." If guilt nags at you for being distant, remember—most people are happy to hear from friends, so no explanation is required.

Creatively share yourself in ways that don't require conversation. Some people share photos from a walk or their dinner, others send links to favorite playlists or podcasts, or text a sketch as a greeting. These gestures show warmth without expecting more than you can give.

If in-person contact feels too much, start with brief exchanges in comfortable settings: greet your barista by name, wave at a neighbor, say thanks to a coworker in person rather than email. Try for one "hello" a day—in line, on your street, in the elevator. You don't have to keep up conversation; just being present helps rebuild trust in being with others.

Connection can also mean quietly sharing space—reading together without talking, sitting on the couch with your own phones, or cooking in the same kitchen in silence. These moments offer comfort without pressure.

If you feel stuck, write down three simple ways you could reach out this week—or use this list for inspiration:

- Text an emoji or GIF
- Comment "nice!" on someone's post
- Send a photo from your day
- Share a meme or funny video
- Email an article with "Thought of you"
- Drop off cookies or flowers for a neighbor
- Call and leave a short voicemail
- Reply "thanks" to any message, no matter how late
- Smile at someone in line

- Invite someone for coffee with ZERO obligation to stay if it's too much

Reconnecting after trauma isn't about jumping back into social life. It's about gentle experiments that reassure your nervous system that you can be seen and stay safe. Every small attempt counts—even if it's just hitting "send" on a single emoji.

Support Groups and Peer Communities—What to Expect

Joining a trauma recovery support group—online or in person—can initially feel daunting, as if all eyes are on you or as though you're invisible. You might picture a circle of strangers waiting to judge or dissect your story, but most groups use a simple, predictable format that quickly eases those fears. Meetings generally start with a check-in where members briefly share their mood or weekly experiences. This is followed by an optional round of sharing. Some meetings focus on certain topics, such as managing flashbacks or navigating holidays, while others have an open discussion for whatever members want to bring up. A skilled facilitator or moderator keeps things running smoothly, gently noticing if anyone needs extra support or a pause.

The true value of support groups lies in realizing you aren't as alone as you think. Hearing others describe the same patterns—self-doubt, guilt over boundaries, or sudden tears—can be a tremendous relief. Many people feel a heavy weight lifted when a stranger echoes their own struggles. For example, one person who'd long felt broken after "relapsing" into old habits was surprised to hear their experience described by another group member nearly word-for-word. This didn't resolve everything at once, but it broke down the sense of isolation: "If they aren't monsters for struggling, maybe I'm not either." That's the power of normalization—your pain becomes a shared human experience, not a personal failing.

Groups don't only offer emotional comfort. They provide practical tools as well. You can listen and learn how others set boundaries or voice needs without apology. Some meetings teach grounding exercises, like tracing an object with your eyes or focusing on breathing, to help when anxiety spikes. Members often discuss how to handle life's challenges—dealing with nosy relatives, responding to microaggressions at work, or calming panic attacks on public transport. Every shared story adds another tool to your personal toolkit.

Attending a group for the first time is rarely easy. You might worry about being judged, fear becoming overwhelmed, or feel you have nothing significant to share. Many people just listen at first, which is completely acceptable and seen as participation in most trauma-informed communities. You won't be pressured to talk until you're ready, and if the discussion stirs up tough emotions, it's fine to step away—mute your mic, turn off your camera, or leave the meeting as you need. There's no pressure to justify your feelings.

To calm nerves before joining, try grounding yourself—breathe slowly, have something comforting nearby, and remind yourself there are no emotional "requirements." Give yourself permission to simply observe if that's all you can do. Feeling triggered or overwhelmed by someone else's story is natural; there's no need for self-judgment.

The choice of which group to attend matters. Look for trauma-informed facilitators—people skilled at creating safe, respectful environments and intervening if emotions run high. Good groups have clear, posted guidelines: strict confidentiality, no pressure to disclose, and an emphasis on respect. Accessibility can vary—some groups meet in person, others online (video optional), and some allow anonymous chat participation. Flexible formats exist for those with unpredictable schedules, including drop-in meetings or asynchronous forums.

Watch for warning signs. Avoid groups that push you to share before you're comfortable, or imply that talking is the only path to healing. If facilitators gossip, members "diagnose" one another, or peer support is being promoted as a replacement for professional help, look elsewhere. Trust your instincts—if a group leaves you feeling more upset than comforted, it's okay to move on.

It may take trying several groups to find the right fit. Some people prefer general groups; others look for those specific to their faith, gender identity, age, or trauma type. Online forums can feel safer for newcomers, allowing you to just read for weeks before posting, while in-person groups offer warmth but may feel more vulnerable. Each format has its pros and cons.

Every group develops its own personality and rhythm. Don't be discouraged if the first ones you try aren't right for you. Keep exploring until you find a space where you feel at ease—whether quietly listening or speaking up. Over time, support groups and peer communities can become places where you not only reconnect with others but also rebuild trust in your ability to be heard and understood.

Navigating "Old" Relationships with Your "New" Self

Rebuilding your identity after trauma brings challenges, especially with long-standing relationships. You may change in ways those closest to you don't expect—or even resist. This shift can be both hopeful and heartbreaking, often feeling like you're speaking a new language while friends or family hold onto an outdated version of you. There's a quiet grief in realizing some connections can't keep up with your growth, or that loved ones might not recognize who you're becoming. Old patterns, roles, and unspoken rules may pull at you, tempting you to revert to your former self. It's normal to feel uncertain, frustrated, or lonely as you renegotiate your place in relationships that once felt secure.

As you set new boundaries or voice different needs, old friends or relatives may react with confusion or suspicion. They might question, "What happened to you?" or claim you "used to be so easygoing," not realizing ease often meant self-sacrifice. These reactions can sting, and you may grieve the loss of shared laughter or the comfort of being known. At the same time, you might begin to see how much of your old self was shaped by survival—agreeing when you meant no, tolerating hurtful behavior, or hiding parts of yourself to avoid conflict. Even positive change can feel awkward as it means stepping into unknown territory.

Communicating new boundaries and needs requires courage and practice. Be direct but gentle: "I'm working on things in therapy and may need different things," or "This is important for my well-being." You don't owe lengthy explanations; a simple statement suffices, like, "I'm learning to take better care of myself, which means I need more space sometimes," or, "Certain topics are hard for me right now, so I'd like to focus on other things." If someone pushes past your limits, stand firm: "I know this is new for you, but I really need you to respect this."

Expect some pushback. People may become defensive ("Are

you saying I'm the problem?"), minimize your changes ("You're overreacting"), or reminisce about "the old you," hoping you'll revert. Often, their discomfort is about the changes themselves. If a conversation gets tense or you feel yourself slipping into old roles—agreeing when you don't mean to or apologizing for having needs—take a pause: "I need a break to think about this," or "Let's pause for now." Brief time-outs interrupt old patterns and give space to both sides.

Sometimes, a relationship adapts; people may surprise you by stepping up. Other times, the gap widens and connections can't survive. This isn't failure—it's a sign you're honoring your authentic self above familiarity or obligation.

Letting go or redefining relationships is bittersweet. Guilt may tug at you for stepping back from friends or relatives who won't respect boundaries. But enduring pain isn't loyalty; it's self-abandonment. Ask yourself honestly: Which relationships bring energy and support? Which leave you drained or doubting? Try listing connections that nurture versus those that sap your spirit. Notice patterns, but don't pressure yourself to act immediately.

Grieving lost relationships is part of the process. If it's hard to express, try writing a goodbye letter (even if you don't send it). Acknowledge what you wish they understood, what you're grateful for, and what still hurts. Naming the loss helps make space for healing and future connections.

Moving forward doesn't always mean cutting people out. You might just see someone less often, change what you talk about, or lean more on chosen family—those who support the real you. The goal isn't perfect relationships but alignment with your evolving self.

When it feels like your world is shrinking because old ties no longer fit, keep seeking those who see and support you. New connections—whether through shared interests, support groups, or unexpected friendships—emerge as you honor your authentic self. Trust that the space created by letting go will eventually fill with new warmth and belonging.

Remember this: Reclaiming your identity after trauma changes not just how you show up for yourself, but also how you relate to others. The process can sting and bring unexpected grief, yet it opens the door to honesty and deeper relationships. In the next chapter, we'll explore shaping a hopeful future, grounded in self-trust and the wisdom gained from these changes.

*Throughout my journey, I've experienced both deeply supportive relationships and others that left me feeling unseen or unheard. Letting go of long-standing connections—even when those relationships fail to honor my boundaries or offer the understanding I need—has been one of the hardest parts of my healing process. In my previous book, *When the Church Thinks You're Crazy,* I delve further into this challenge. For me, finding clarity took time: sifting through my thoughts and feelings, allowing myself to grieve, and gradually making decisions that prioritized my sense of safety and well-being.*

10. Future Visualization and Planning

Meeting Your Future Self: Guided Visualization Exercise

After trauma, hope can seem fragile or distant. Looking ahead may feel impossible or pointless when your past has left you feeling lost. However, imagining a future self—someone who has survived and even grown—can be quietly transformative. Future-self visualization isn't about fantasy or perfection; it's about gently reminding yourself that change is possible, even if slow or unpredictable. This practice gives you permission to picture what healing could look like for you, one detail at a time.

You can do this exercise however you like—eyes closed, open, sitting, lying down, or standing by a window. Begin by picturing a place that feels safe and comfortable, real or imagined: maybe a sunlit room, beneath a familiar tree, or a longed-for destination. Take in the little details: the colors, background sounds, the air's temperature. Allow yourself to feel present in this space. Now, envision someone approaching—that person is you, one year or several years from now. Their image may be blurry at first, which is okay. With each breath, let their outline become a bit clearer. Observe this future-you: their stance, their smile, how relaxed or confident they appear. Notice their clothing, posture, and how they breathe or use their hands.

Pay attention to the emotions coming from this future self. Do they radiate calm, warmth, or certainty? Is there a sense of peace or ease? Maybe they appear more comfortable in their own skin. If this future self is hard to picture, any image—even the faintest impression—counts. Quietly, ask this version of you: "What do you want me to know about healing and about who I am becoming?" The answer may be words, a feeling, a memory, or even just silence. Messages might be simple—"Keep going," "You're doing better than you think," "Rest is not failure"—or might come as an image or sensation. Stay open to whatever comes.

Afterward, jot down your impressions in a journal, sketchbook, or notes app. Capture what stood out—how your future self looked, what emotions you sensed, or any communications that arose. If writing is tough, doodle shapes or lines matching the feeling. You might even create a collage using images, symbols, and colors that evoke the sense of this future-you.

Interactive Prompt: Anchoring Your Future-Self Vision

Answer these prompts after your visualization:

- What did your future self look like? Any small details—clothing, jewelry, hairstyle?
- How did they move? Did anything about their posture feel new or different?
- What feeling did they give off? Can you sum it up in one word?
- Did your future self say anything? If not, what do you wish they'd said?

If drawing comes more naturally than writing, sketch what you saw—even simple stick figures can be meaningful. If speaking feels easier, record a voice memo describing the experience.

Mixed emotions are common after this exercise—hope, excitement, grief, or skepticism all have a place. It's normal to feel relief or frustration if the vision is unclear. If your future self seems far away, focus on a single detail: a color, a sound, the way they stood. These small fragments still matter and show that you're willing to consider change.

Even if your image of the future is incomplete or unclear, note whatever stands out. Healing doesn't need perfect understanding—sometimes all you need is a small flicker of hope to move forward.

Setting Gentle, Attainable Goals—No More Self-Sabotage

Goal-setting can feel daunting if you've experienced trauma. Years of survival mode may make "goals" seem like just another area to fail. Maybe you've tried lists, vision boards, or strict routines, then dropped them when life got hard. This isn't due to laziness or brokenness; it's that traditional goal-setting ignores what trauma has taught your mind and body—self-protection takes priority, and big changes can feel unsafe. Goals need to be gentle invitations, not rigid demands.

You deserve a compassionate approach to goals—one that matches your pace, allows for tough days, and lets you adjust course without guilt. Healing goals aren't about perfection but about moving toward what matters, in small, manageable steps. Treat goals as flexible guides rooted in your values, reflecting what feels possible right now. For example, if you crave connection but feel isolated, your first goal could simply be to read a friend's message, even if you don't respond. If self-care is tough, your goal could be to notice when you're thirsty or tired. There's no right size or speed.

Big dreams often overwhelm, so breaking them into micro-goals can help progress feel safer. Imagine a ladder: the highest rung is your big hope—maybe feeling more connected or finding meaningful work. The lowest rung is the smallest step you can manage today, like scrolling through your contacts or reading old messages if you want to reconnect with people. The next step could be drafting a text, even if you don't send it. Each small action counts. This "laddering" technique makes even large hopes feel doable by turning them into simple, realistic actions. Progress is about small advances, especially when bold moves aren't possible.

Self-sabotage often appears when you start something new. You might set a goal, then procrastinate, criticize your efforts, or avoid the goal. Perfectionism might tell you that if you can't do it perfectly, you shouldn't bother trying. Overwhelm can hit when goals seem too big, and avoidance claims, "it's not the right time." These are survival habits, not moral failings. Think back: when have you given up on a goal before? Was the bar set too high? Did you expect too much from yourself, too soon? Did shame or exhaustion cause you to stop after a setback? Reflecting on these patterns isn't self-blame—it's understanding what got in your way, so you can plan differently now.

When self-sabotage returns (and it will), self-compassion is essential. Remind yourself, "This is harder than I thought," or "I'm allowed to start over as often as I need." It's okay to return to an old goal after taking a break, or to walk away from one that doesn't fit anymore. Quitting isn't failing—it's self-awareness. Maybe you wanted to journal nightly but stopped after a tough week. That's not failure; your needs simply changed. Maybe weekly voice memos or brief phone notes feel easier for now.

Gentle check-ins keep goals helpful and not stressful. Once a week—or once a month if that suits you—ask what's working and what isn't. Does this goal feel supportive or punishing? Do you need to shrink it, stretch it, or swap it out? If a goal brings dread or shame, it's time to adjust it without apology. Regular reviews should be about kindness and flexibility—not matching someone else's standards. Sometimes, letting go of a goal requires more courage than sticking with it.

Return to your values as your compass. Your original plan may not fit anymore—your energy or priorities might have shifted, which is normal and healthy during trauma recovery. You're allowed to adjust your course as often as needed. What matters most is that your goals serve you, not the other way around.

Tracking Progress with Visual Tools and Journals

Change often arrives so quietly that it's easy to miss—especially for trauma survivors, whose progress can feel invisible and slow. This invisibility can sap motivation, making it hard to notice any payoff in the work you're doing. That's where visual tools and journals come in. They aren't about proving anything to others, but helping you see, honor, and sometimes even celebrate moments of growth that might otherwise go unnoticed. The key is to choose tools that spark interest instead of dread—avoid anything that feels like another obligation. Healing isn't one-size-fits-all, and neither should your tracking methods be.

Tracking progress can be as basic as a paper or app-based habit tracker. Draw a series of boxes for each day or week, filling them in whenever you accomplish something meaningful—drinking water, reaching out to someone, or taking a mindful breath. Or try a progress jar: each time you achieve a micro-win (like setting a boundary or finishing a tough task), drop a bead or stone into a jar. The growing weight and sound become tangible proof of your effort over time.

For the visually inclined, vision boards and "future-self" collages offer creative alternatives. Clip images, words, or colors from magazines representing who or how you want to be. It's not about making the perfect poster, but letting your subconscious guide you toward hope or comfort with whatever images call to you.

Bullet journals provide another flexible framework. Use them to create simple checklists, track moods, or maintain "feeling meters" with color-coded emotions: blue for calm, yellow for anxious, green for connection. If you enjoy drawing, print out a blank image—a tree, mandala, or calendar—and color in a section each time you take a healing step. These small coloring rituals make progress visible while offering pockets of mindfulness.

Reflection and Ritual

Weekly reflection prompts can deepen your tracking. Try asking, "What did I learn about myself this week?" or "How did I honor my values today?" Your answers can be brief—sometimes bullet points or half-sentences say more than full paragraphs. Another helpful prompt: "What felt easier than before?"—maybe you set a boundary more readily, or found yourself laughing more often. Noticing what's changing helps train your attention on growth, not just gaps.

Interactive rituals can make tracking less isolating and more meaningful. If you feel safe, share a photo of your colored tracker or vision board with a friend, or mention your progress by text. Some online support groups have "progress threads" for sharing small victories with people who understand. Even telling one person can provide warmth and a sense of accountability.

Adding simple rituals to milestones adds depth. Light a candle when you complete a tracker or reach a micro-goal, or play your favorite song after you fill your progress jar halfway. Write a quick congratulatory note to yourself and tuck it in your journal. These aren't about major celebrations; they're quiet acknowledgments, giving yourself a moment to feel satisfied with progress—no matter how small.

The real reward of visual tracking and journaling is the story that builds over time. On tough days, looking back at a full jar, colorful chart, or pages of reflections can remind you that things are changing, even when progress feels invisible. These methods are tangible proof of your efforts, showing that small actions accumulate and you are moving forward—even if no one else yet notices.

Reclaiming Joy and Passion: Rebuilding What Trauma Took

Rediscovering joy after trauma can feel nearly impossible—sometimes even forbidden. Many say they miss feeling pleasure in small things—a favorite song, a cold drink, or a laugh with a friend. Others describe an emotional numbness that colors everything gray. Old hobbies or dreams can cause a painful ache, leaving you uncertain if you're grieving a loss or just protecting yourself. This blend of longing, grief, and hesitation around reclaiming joy is valid and normal. After profound pain, even thinking about happiness may feel risky or unfamiliar; you are not alone in this.

The sadness over lost interests is part of healing, not a sign you're stuck. Former passions like drawing, swimming, or baking might now seem pointless or dull. Maybe your dreams feel unreachable, and even getting through the week is hard. Trauma often mutes life's vibrancy, making old sources of happiness hard to pursue. Hesitation about joy is common; sometimes it seems suspicious, even unsafe, to feel happy after suffering.

Where to begin when joy feels out of reach? Start small, giving yourself permission to try things with no pressure. Create a "joy menu": jot down things that once made you smile or things you're even slightly curious about. These can be as simple as the smell of fresh bread, watering a plant, doodling, watching a show, or enjoying some sunshine. Circle what feels most accessible and try one this week—no expectations, just a gentle test to see if anything resonates.

Approach this as a scavenger hunt, not a test. Each week, revisit an old pastime or try something new—sample a recipe, move to music for a minute, or stroll in a nearby park. This isn't about instantly finding a lifelong passion, but rather gently allowing your mind and body chances to reconnect with pleasure. If things still feel flat or disappointing, that's okay; it often takes time to truly experience enjoyment again.

Bring some playfulness to the process, even if it feels awkward at first. Recall a time you felt playful—what were you doing, and can you recreate a sliver of that sensation? If not, what's the smallest playful step you can manage now? Sometimes, having company helps. Find a "joy buddy" who also wants to rediscover pleasure; check in, swap ideas, or try things together via text or video.

Honor your pace. Some activities might require several attempts before they evoke any true feeling. Be gentle with yourself if joy is slow to emerge or if something fails to delight. Fun doesn't come easily after hardship, but give yourself credit for simply showing up and making the effort.

There are many ways people rediscover passion. Some find unexpected calm in gardening, others in painting, or volunteering. Joy can slip in through small, unplanned moments. For one person, working at an animal shelter brought a surprise sense of usefulness and happiness, even when they didn't expect it. Sometimes joy finds you sideways, when you're not searching for it directly.

To explore further, jot down a list of activities, old or new, that might bring you joy. Include "wild ideas"—things you'd like to try, even if you never have before. Each week, pick one. There's no failure if you don't enjoy it. Just experimenting means hope and curiosity are still there.

Allow your sense of joy to evolve—sometimes it's quiet, sometimes unexpectedly bright. Each attempt matters, even if it ends in disappointment. The simple act of seeking pleasure again is an act of courage and self-respect.

When Dreams Change—Permission to Evolve

Sometimes the dreams and goals you carried for years simply stop fitting. Maybe you wake up and realize that what once lit you up now feels distant, or you notice a gentle disinterest where there used to be fire. This isn't a crisis or a sign that you're failing at recovery. In truth, one of the healthiest things you can do is allow your dreams to change shape as you heal. Growth after trauma often looks like letting go of old blueprints so something more honest can take root. There's nothing shameful about outgrowing what used to matter—even if you spent a long time chasing it. Old dreams might fall away, leaving a sense of emptiness or grief, but this space is fertile ground for something new.

Outgrowing an old identity or ambition is not the same as quitting. It's more like shedding a skin that no longer protects you. Sometimes, this means grieving not just the dream, but the person you thought you'd become. You might feel sadness for the years spent moving toward a goal that now seems misaligned with who you are. For instance, I remember supporting someone who had poured years into a career path, only to realize after deep healing work that the job was built on values that no longer matched their heart. At first, there was disappointment and confusion. Eventually, though, there was relief and a renewed sense of possibility.

Grieving what no longer fits is an act of self-respect. It's okay to honor the things you're leaving behind—even if they never fully materialized. You might find it helpful to write a "goodbye letter" to an old goal or version of yourself. Pour out the feelings: gratitude for what it taught you, sorrow for what never was, and relief for the freedom to move on. Consider this reflection: "What dream have I let go of, and what is starting to fill the space it left behind?" If writing isn't your style, speak your goodbye out loud or use art—draw, paint, or collage the shift from old to new.

Fresh desires tend to stir quietly at first. Maybe there's a flicker of curiosity about something unexpected—a field you never considered, a skill you want to explore, a type of connection that feels different from old patterns. Even if these new possibilities seem odd or out of reach, pay attention. Tuning in doesn't mean committing right away. Instead, ask yourself: "What's one thing my future self might want—even if I'm not ready to want it yet?" Curiosity is a sign of life returning. It's perfectly normal for these new ideas to feel both exciting and scary; unfamiliar territory always brings a mix of hope and doubt.

Sometimes it helps to give yourself an actual "permission slip" to want something new. Write it down: "I give myself permission to let go of what doesn't fit anymore and to explore what might." Pin it somewhere visible or keep it in your wallet as a gentle nudge when old guilt or fear creeps in.

Authenticity isn't about sticking with every dream you've ever had; it's about letting your life reflect who you are now—not who you were in survival mode or who others expected you to be. Evolving dreams are evidence that you're living honestly and honoring your growth. There's no starting over—just moving forward with new information and deeper self-understanding.

Sidebar: Authenticity means changing as you heal—your future self is yours to create.

Remember this: dreams are allowed to shift as your healing deepens. You don't have to force yourself into old roles or chase outdated goals. Making space for new ambitions is not just okay—it's a powerful step toward reclaiming your real identity. In the next chapter, we'll focus on weaving support and community into this new vision of yourself, because nobody heals in isolation.

Envisioning my future self and reigniting my sense of passion have been deeply intertwined with my spiritual connection to God. Through prayer, I brought my questions—both the ones I struggled to answer and the ones I was afraid to ask—into that sacred space. I learned to listen quietly, trusting that God understood my needs more fully than I ever could on my own. Over the years, I have continued this practice of intentional, heartfelt prayer—asking, listening, and waiting. Choosing this path transformed my life from overwhelming chaos and pain to a state of profound calm, peace, and joy. I am truly grateful for this spiritual foundation, which has anchored my healing and guided me toward a more authentic and hope-filled future.

11. Integrating Faith, Community, and Growth

The Value of Prayer and Spiritual Practices for Grounding Truth

In trauma recovery, it often feels like there's no solid ground. When pain lingers, people frequently reach for prayer or spiritual practices—not because every answer is clear, but because they need something steady amid turmoil. Spiritual practices aren't about performance; they're a means of finding presence and pausing when trauma threatens to steal it.

Prayer, whether spoken, whispered, written, or silent, helps regulate the nervous system—something science is starting to confirm. In moments of anxiety or shame, repeating a phrase or sitting in intentional silence can calm your body and mind. Prayer doesn't need elaborate words; "Help," "Thank you," or simply sitting quietly and noticing your breath can be enough. Spiritual rituals—lighting a candle, bowing your head, holding a small object—allow hope to become physical, grounding you in the present. Research from the National Center for PTSD supports this, showing spiritual practices are linked to better trauma coping by providing connection, meaning, and hope during uncertainty (see APA list, source 10).

The difference between performative and authentic spiritual practice is key. Performative spirituality, done out of habit or expectation, can become empty. Authentic spiritual practice, however, nourishes and connects you to a loving God. You don't need to follow a script or go to a special place; authenticity matters more than tradition.

Sometimes, what once worked spiritually no longer does, and that's okay—it's a sign of growth, not failure. Allow yourself to adapt or reimagine rituals to fit your needs. If old prayers now trigger pain, step back or skip them. If group worship feels unsafe, it's fine to keep your practice private or experiment with new forms. Faith can be solitary, shared, structured, or spontaneous. Some find comfort in traditional liturgy; others prefer walking outdoors or journaling as their way of encountering the sacred.

Beyond traditional prayer, other spiritual activities can offer powerful grounding. Breath prayers are simple yet effective: pairing your inhalations and exhalations with phrases like "Peace in" and "Fear out." This practice unites body and spirit, easing anxiety and spiritual hunger. Meditative walking—moving slowly and focusing on each step as a silent prayer—can also bring peace. Lighting a candle becomes a ritual for pausing and remembering what matters. Journaling as prayer—writing letters to God—allows you to express questions and burdens.

Creating sacred space at home can be simple: a corner with comforting objects, a verse, stones from meaningful walks, or other hopeful symbols. The space doesn't need to follow any tradition unless that feels grounding; it only needs to feel safe and personal. When life is overwhelming, even a short return to this space can restore calm.

Trauma can disrupt our trust in faith traditions and spiritual communities. Many survivors confront spiritual wounds: doubt, anger at God, unsettled beliefs. If you're struggling with faith after trauma, know you're not alone—it's a common, human response. It's normal to feel angry or question everything. These responses are valid.

A gentle way to process these wounds is journaling—writing "letters to God," venting doubts without self-censorship, or simply naming your questions honestly. Some seek spiritual direction, finding a supportive guide who helps them process beliefs and wounds. Others participate in support groups for those recovering from spiritual trauma, sharing stories and hearing their own echoed by others.

For example, "Renee" felt disconnected from her childhood faith after trauma shattered her trust in people and God. She couldn't bear church or prayer for years. Gradually, with patient support, she started lighting a candle each morning—not as a belief, but as a hope ritual. She wrote letters to God she never meant to send. Eventually, she found peace by creating new grounding routines appropriate for her healing journey, not by returning to old ones.

Interactive Reflection: Exploring Your Spiritual Comfort Zone

Take a quiet moment to consider:

- Which spiritual practices have brought comfort before—even briefly?
- Are any rituals or prayers now heavy or unsafe?
- What new forms of spiritual expression might feel safe enough to try?
- If you could create your own grounding ritual (with no rules), what would it include?

Write down any words, images, objects, or songs that emerge, without worrying if they're "spiritual enough."

Give yourself permission to build new habits slowly, release what no longer serves you, and trust that faith and identity can be reimagined as you heal (see APA list, source 10).

Integrating Scripture as a Source of Identity and Hope

Scripture is more than a list of rules or childhood memory verses—it can be a source of comfort, affirmation, and renewal, especially for those whose experiences with it have included obligation or even harm. For many, especially survivors of trauma, approaching scripture can be fraught, often stirring up confusion or guilt instead of solace. If this resonates with you, remember: you're allowed to engage with scripture on your own terms. It need not be a test, but a wellspring for honest encouragement and healing.

When trauma distorts your sense of self, certain verses can serve as anchors, grounding you in truths that outlast circumstance. Try reading through the lens of affirmation rather than doctrinal correctness. For instance, Psalm 34:18 assures, "The Lord is close to the brokenhearted and saves those who are crushed in spirit." This isn't a demand to heal yourself, but an assurance you're not alone at your lowest. Similarly, Isaiah 43:1 says, "Do not fear, for I have redeemed you; I have called you by name, you are mine," offering belonging amid shame or isolation. Second Corinthians 5:17 reminds: "If anyone is in Christ, the new creation has come: The old has gone, the new is here!"—a gentle promise of transformation, not erasure of the past.

You don't have to be a theologian—or even religious—to

benefit from scripture's nourishing side. Sometimes, the power of these texts comes from making them personal. Psalm 139:14 declares, "I praise you because I am fearfully and wonderfully made." If that feels hard to believe, rewrite it in your voice, like "I am made with care and purpose." Place your version somewhere visible—a sticky note or your phone lock screen—so it can stand against internalized shame a little each day.

Creative interaction with scripture can help bypass old barriers and resistance. Choose gentle, inviting verses and experiment with writing them in bold letters or comforting colors. Sketch images inspired by a passage, arrange meaningful words in a collage, or rephrase a verse as a letter to yourself—"You are beloved. Your life matters." This isn't about perfection, but allowing small truths about your value to settle in over time.

Let scripture become part of your daily rhythm in ways that soothe and empower you. Simple breath prayers with scripture phrases—inhale "Peace," exhale "Be still"—offer calm in anxious moments. Repeat short verses quietly, letting them settle into your heartbeat. Try lectio divina: read a verse slowly several times, noticing what word or phrase draws you in, then pause and wonder, "What does this say to me today?" Even a few minutes can make scripture feel more like a companion than a challenge.

Scripture journaling is another gentle path. Write out a verse, and jot down what stands out—or what confuses or upsets you. Ask what it evokes in you: tension, comfort, anger? There are no wrong answers. One day a verse may offer nothing; another day, it might spark fresh hope. The point isn't to force a lesson, but to meet scripture with honesty.

Many people, understandably, carry wounds from spiritual abuse or harmful interpretations of scripture. Some verses may have been used to silence or shame. Others can trigger lingering pain. If so, your response is valid—set aside verses that hurt and focus instead on those that bring relief or clarity. Consider trauma-informed devotionals and Bible studies designed for survivors, which avoid shaming language and center on gentleness and curiosity.

For instance, one person once braced herself for Ephesians 5 in church, as it had been used to justify control. But she discovered Galatians 5:1: "It is for freedom that Christ has set us free." That verse became her mantra in therapy, easing the grip of weaponized passages and affirming her dignity and freedom.

If scripture has hurt you before, take it slow. Journaling your responses—anger, confusion, grief—can help loosen the hold of painful verses.

Scripture doesn't belong exclusively to any tradition or leader. It can be a living resource for anyone seeking hope after trauma. The goal isn't to memorize the most verses, but to discover even one small phrase safe enough to hold onto when everything feels shaky.

Trauma-Sensitive Verses for Reflection

Here are a few passages to explore—read them slowly and notice if any offer comfort:

- Psalm 34:18 – The Lord is close to the brokenhearted.
- Isaiah 43:1 – I have called you by name; you are mine.

- Psalm 139:14 – You are fearfully and wonderfully made.
- Zephaniah 3:17 – The Lord rejoices over you with singing.
- Matthew 11:28 – Come to me, all who are weary.
- 2 Corinthians 5:17 – The new creation has come.

You might copy one of these into your journal, rewrite it as a note to yourself, or simply sit quietly with the words. There's no right way—just whatever brings a flicker of reassurance or peace.

Building Your Personal Support Network—Faith, Friends, and Beyond

When you're healing from trauma, one of the most important things you can do—though sometimes the hardest—is to look at who's around you. Who do you lean on? Who really sees you? Who drains you or leaves you feeling small, and who helps you remember your strength? Your support network isn't just about who sits with you in a crisis; it's everyone, from a neighbor who checks in to the mentor who listens when things get rough. Mapping this out can feel intimidating at first, but it turns confusion into clarity and gives you a visual picture of where support is strong and where it's missing.

Start by grabbing a piece of paper and drawing a big circle in the middle. This is your "circle of support." Write your name in the center, then add names or roles in rings around you. Include family, friends, faith leaders, neighbors, mentors, therapists, and even community resources like support groups, helplines, or local organizations. If you're more digital, make a quick chart or note on your phone. Don't worry if your circle feels sparse—quality matters more than quantity. This audit isn't about blame; it's about seeing what's real right now.

Now take an honest inventory. Who do you contact when you need encouragement? Who do you reach out to for practical help—rides, meals, advice? Who listens without judgment? Are there people who offer spiritual support or connection? Be specific. Maybe your aunt texts Bible verses when you're down, or your old college roommate always makes space for your feelings. Include professionals too—a therapist is part of your network even if you see them only once a month.

Once your list is down, it helps to evaluate each connection. Who feels safe and nurturing? Who leaves you feeling heavy or anxious? Sometimes people we've known for years no longer fit the role we wish they did, and that's okay to admit. Notice patterns: maybe you have plenty of practical help, but feel lonely for emotional support. Maybe spiritual community feels thin, or friendship is abundant, but professional support is missing. This isn't about shame—it's about gathering information so you can decide where to strengthen or shift things.

If your network feels thin or unreliable, it might be time to seek out new connections. Reaching out is vulnerable work. Start small. If you're considering talking to a faith leader or therapist, think about what would make the conversation feel safe—maybe an email before meeting in person, or a short call to set expectations. You don't have to spill your whole story right away. Sometimes just asking for a coffee chat or saying "I'm having a hard time lately" is enough to open a door. When approaching someone new—whether it's for spiritual guidance, therapy, or just peer support—remember that the best supporters respect your boundaries and timing.

Setting up regular check-ins with your support people can anchor relationships during tough times. You might schedule a weekly call with a friend or plan monthly meetups with a small group at church, in the neighborhood, or even online. These don't have to be formal; consistency matters more than structure. If you're interested in expanding your network further, try joining interest-based groups like book clubs, volunteer teams, or mutual aid collectives. Shared activities often make connections less intimidating and more meaningful.

As you build out your network, it becomes crucial to discern who truly supports your healing and who does not. Safe supporters share certain traits: reliability—they show up when they say they will; empathy—they listen without judgment or rushing to "fix"; confidentiality—they keep what you share private; encouragement—they celebrate growth without jealousy; and reciprocity—they give and receive without keeping score. Beware of red flags: relationships where emotional manipulation takes root ("If you loved me, you'd…"), chronic judgment or shaming, persistent one-sidedness (you always giving, they always taking), and anyone who pressures you to move faster than feels safe.

It's easy to fall into patterns of only giving or only receiving in relationships—especially after trauma has taught you that love equals self-sacrifice. True support networks thrive on reciprocity and healthy boundaries. Balance is key. Practice both asking for help and offering it—without guilt or expectation of payback. If this feels awkward at first, try using simple scripts: "Would you have time for a phone call this week? I could use some support," or "Thank you for checking in. I really appreciate it." When someone helps you, express gratitude openly; even a quick message matters.

Sometimes it helps to set up a "care team" during especially hard seasons—a handful of people who agree to check in regularly or help with specific needs. I have a friend who made a group chat with three close friends during chemotherapy; they rotated meal drop-offs and texted encouragement on treatment days. She said it felt awkward asking at first, but ended up making her less isolated and more connected than ever before.

As life changes, so will your needs and resources. Consider doing an annual or seasonal review of your support network—what's working well? Where are gaps showing up? Who has drifted away? Are there new faces who could become trusted allies? Adjust as needed; this isn't static. Needs shift as healing deepens.

Remember: building a strong network doesn't mean keeping every relationship forever. It means getting honest about who helps you grow and who doesn't—and honoring that truth with compassion for yourself and others. Support looks different for everyone, but everyone deserves it.

Embracing Lifelong Growth: Living Authentically After Trauma

Healing after trauma doesn't have a finish line; it moves more like the seasons or the growth rings in an old tree. Sometimes, change is fast and wild—new shoots everywhere, a rush of green after rain. At other times, things slow down and you hardly notice anything shifting at all, but deep inside, roots are working, and new possibilities are forming. Your identity is a living garden. There will be stretches of blossom, months of pruning, unexpected weeds, and moments where you just sit quietly in the shade, grateful for a bit of peace. You never "arrive" at some perfect self; instead, you keep tending to what matters, learning what flourishes in your soil, and letting go of what no longer fits.

As you continue forward, regular self-reflection can help you see these changes. Life pulls you in all directions—work, family, responsibilities, memories—and it's easy to lose track of what feels true right now. Setting aside time each month or year to check in with yourself can keep you anchored. You might ask, "What feels most real for me now? What am I longing for? What's changed in how I see myself or the world?" Sometimes the answers will surprise you. Maybe what mattered most last year barely registers today. Perhaps new dreams are taking root, or old interests are fading as you discover fresh passions. This isn't backsliding—this is real growth.

These check-ins don't have to be complicated. Jot your thoughts in a journal, voice record them on your phone, or even share them with a trusted friend or mentor. Over time, you'll notice patterns—recurring values, shifting hopes, lessons learned not from easy days but from moments when things didn't go as planned. Celebrating these shifts matters. Even if the world doesn't notice your quiet progress, you will begin to recognize how much you've changed and how resilient you've become.

Setbacks and new losses will still happen along the way—life doesn't stop testing us just because we've survived one storm. When these moments hit, it's normal to feel like everything's unraveling again. This is where resilience rituals come in handy. Some people mark anniversaries of hard events not with dread, but with small acts of kindness toward themselves—a special meal, a walk in nature, a letter to their younger self. Others celebrate personal "growth milestones" like setting a boundary that once felt impossible or reaching out for support when they once would have shut down.

A "growth journal" can serve as a quiet witness to your evolution. Recording lessons learned from both joy and pain helps capture the texture of your story—not just the highlight reel but the tough stuff too. Maybe you jot down the moment you realized you could say no without guilt or the first time laughter felt real again after months of numbness. Tracking these moments makes it easier to see progress when discouragement creeps in.

Lifelong growth isn't only inward-focused; eventually, many find themselves wanting to give back. Sharing what you've learned can be a powerful act of healing in itself. Some become peer mentors for others starting their recovery process—listening, offering gentle advice, and showing what's possible by their presence alone. Others get involved in advocacy or volunteer with support groups or faith ministries. Even small acts—like comforting a friend who feels lost or writing an encouraging note to someone struggling—can ripple outward and bring unexpected meaning.

I once met a survivor who started as a participant in a trauma recovery group and later became a peer mentor. She said that guiding others made her feel stronger and more whole than she'd ever expected. Her healing deepened as she saw her pain become a source of hope for others. She found that her story wasn't just about survival—it was about helping someone else find their footing on uncertain ground.

Reflecting on what legacy your healing might leave can reframe setbacks and struggles as part of something bigger than yourself. Ask yourself: "What do I want my story to mean? How do I want to shape the world around me because of what I've survived?" You don't need grand gestures; even quiet acts of kindness count.

Sometimes giving back is simply telling your story—to one person, in a journal, or as part of a group—so someone else knows they're not alone. Sometimes it means standing up for others who haven't found their voice yet. Other times it's about modeling self-compassion and healthy boundaries in everyday life, showing that growth isn't about perfection but about staying curious and open.

Lifelong growth asks us to remain flexible and honest with ourselves—to accept that change will come in waves and cycles. There will always be new challenges and uncharted territory. Even so, every lesson learned and every step forward adds another ring to your story—a sign that you are alive and still growing.

Remember this: reclaiming your identity after trauma is not about reaching some fixed endpoint. It's about tending to your own living garden year after year—pausing to notice new blooms, learning from the scars on old branches, and sharing your harvest with others when you're ready. Growth continues, quietly and steadily, no matter what comes next.

In conclusion, we'll look at ways to make room for joy and meaning each day—planting seeds for tomorrow without losing sight of what's possible now.

For many years, I struggled to trust and build friendships. Experiences of betrayal in the past made it difficult to reach out or let people in. What helped me most during that lonely season was turning to prayer. I gently asked God to bring wise, compassionate people into my life—friends I could love and who would truly care for me in return. Over time, my prayers were answered, and a supportive circle has gradually grown around me. These relationships have become a powerful source of healing and connection. Prayer has been a guiding force in every step of my healing journey. My heartfelt prayer for you, dear reader, is that you, too, receive the healing and wholeness that God desires for you. May your future unfold with deep love, lasting peace, and abundant joy.

Conclusion

If you're holding this book and reaching the final pages, I want to pause right here and say: I see you. I know this has not been an easy journey. Every chapter you've read, every exercise you tried (or even just thought about trying), every moment you stayed with discomfort instead of turning away—these are acts of deep courage. Most people never have to question who they are. You've had to fight to reclaim what trauma tried to take, and that takes guts. If you feel tired, uncertain, or proud—or all three at once—know that all those feelings belong here.

My hope in writing this book was never to draw a straight line from pain to perfection. I wanted to walk beside you as you learned to trust yourself again, bit by bit. I want to say it out loud, one more time: It is possible to reclaim your real, authentic self after trauma. You are not destined to remain lost or stuck. Healing isn't a quick fix or a straight path, but it is real, and it's absolutely worth every shaky, messy, or hopeful step you take.

Let's look back at the ground you've covered. In the beginning, we named what trauma does to identity—the emptiness, the "Who am I now?" moments, the confusion that can settle into your bones. We explored how identity loss isn't a weakness; it's a sign your mind and body did their best to protect you. You learned that your pain is valid, even if the world hasn't always seen or believed it.

We talked about the common traps: failed solutions that promised quick fixes, the urge to blame yourself when those didn't work, and the weight of shame and self-doubt. Together, we built a new map—the Identity Reconstruction Roadmap. This map isn't rigid. It's a flexible guide designed to honor your pace, your background, and your needs. You discovered ways to rediscover your likes and dislikes, clarify what you care about, and try small experiments to reconnect with joy and interest.

We walked through mind-body tools—grounding, breathwork, and gentle movement—to help you return to yourself when the world feels overwhelming. You learned self-reparenting and self-compassion practices, giving yourself the care you may have missed before. We practiced saying no, building boundaries, and handling the guilt and pushback that often follow.

We explored what it means to connect with others—how to spot safe people, make micro-connections, and gently step back into community. You learned how to imagine your future self, set gentle goals, and track even the tiniest signs of progress. We talked about weaving faith and spirituality into healing, honoring your story, and building a support network that reflects who you are now. And finally, we circled back to lifelong growth—because healing is a journey, not a destination.

If you take only a handful of truths from these pages, let it be this: You are not broken, and you are not alone. Your pace is valid. Progress might look like a thousand micro-wins and just as many setbacks, but every step counts. Self-compassion is not a luxury—it's a foundation. Boundaries are not selfish—they are necessary. Authentic connection—with God, with yourself, with others- is not just possible. It's your birthright.

You will have days when old wounds sting, when you doubt if you're moving forward at all. That's not failure. That's being human. The spiral of healing means you might revisit old pain, but each time, you do so with new skills, more awareness, and a little more kindness for yourself. Keep this in mind: every time you return to your practices—whether it's journaling, grounding, breathwork, or reaching out for support—you are choosing hope. That's what matters.

These exercises, visual trackers, and reflection prompts are yours to use and adapt. Come back to them as often as you need. Healing is not a one-and-done deal; it's a cycle, and it will look different as you grow. You don't have to do this alone, either. Reach out for support—whether it's a friend, a group, a therapist, or a faith community. Share your story with safe people. And if, one day, you're ready, consider being a beacon for someone else who is feeling lost. There's real power in knowing you can offer the compassion you once needed.

I want you to remember, with every fiber of your being, that you are worthy. Worthy of healing, worthy of joy, worthy of real, lasting connection. It is worth it to say yes and no on your own terms. Worthy of a future where your story and your identity are not defined by trauma, but by the hope and truth you are building right now. There is no finish line, but there is a life ahead—one that is shaped by your choices, your values, and your courage.

Thank you for trusting me and these pages to walk this part of the journey with you. It's an honor I do not take lightly. I hope you carry forward the self-compassion, courage, and hope you've cultivated here—into every new chapter, every setback, and every victory ahead. Your story isn't over. In fact, there are so many good chapters still to come.

As you walk this path toward reclaiming your true identity, please know that you are held in my thoughts and prayers. I truly believe there is hope and healing available for you. Your life is unique, and your story has meaning—not only for yourself, but for others who may one day need your encouragement. I gently invite you to explore where God might be present in your journey and to ask: What does He want you to know right now? Trust that you are not alone, and that restoration is possible.

If you are looking for something deeper—community, support, transformation-something to keep you grounded after reading Reclaiming Your REAL Identity, then join me and others at Bethanyelle.com/realwomen

References

- *The sense of self in the aftermath of trauma - PubMed Central* https://pmc.ncbi.nlm.nih.gov/articles/PMC7594748/
- *The Neuroscience of Dissociation* https://www.psychologytoday.com/us/blog/an-interpersonal-lens/202502/the-neuroscience-of-dissociation
- *IFS Institute: What is Internal Family Systems?* https://ifs-institute.com/
- *C-PTSD Quotes: Inspiring Words on Complex Post-Traumatic* ... https://www.ourmental.health/trauma/insightful-expressions-on-complex-posttraumatic-stress-disorder
- *Identity After Trauma | CPTSDfoundation.org* https://cptsdfoundation.org/2023/05/05/identity-after-trauma/
- *Recognizing the Impact of Big T and Little T Trauma* https://www.psychologytoday.com/us/blog/the-discomfort-zone/202407/recognizing-the-impact-of-big-t-and-little-t-trauma
- *Neuroplasticity after Traumatic Brain Injury* https://www.ncbi.nlm.nih.gov/books/NBK326735/
- *4 Steps for Trauma Survivors to Decrease Self-Blame* https://www.psychologytoday.com/us/blog/invisible-bruises/202405/4-steps-for-trauma-survivors-to-decrease-self-blame

- *6 Common Myths of Self-Help Trauma Recovery Books* https://www.psychologytoday.com/us/blog/simplifying-complex-trauma/202309/6-common-myths-of-self-help-trauma-recovery-books
- *Trauma-Informed Practice (TIP) – Resources* https://www2.gov.bc.ca/gov/content/health/managing-your-health/mental-health-substance-use/child-teen-mental-health/trauma-informed-practice-resources
- *Culturally Informed Trauma and Grief Recovery Toolkit* https://www.apa.org/about/governance/president/grief-toolkit
- *Create Your Personal Safety Plan* https://www.thehotline.org/plan-for-safety/create-your-personal-safety-plan/
- *23 Post Traumatic Growth Worksheets for Therapy (+PDF)* https://positivepsychology.com/post-traumatic-growth-worksheets/
- *23 Post Traumatic Growth Worksheets for Therapy (+PDF)* https://positivepsychology.com/post-traumatic-growth-worksheets/
- *Why Setbacks in Recovery Are a Normal Part of the Process* https://www.harmonyridgerecovery.com/why-setbacks-in-recovery-are-a-normal-part-of-the-process/
- *23 Post Traumatic Growth Worksheets for Therapy (+PDF)* https://positivepsychology.com/post-traumatic-growth-worksheets/

- *Involuntary Memories and Dissociative Amnesia* https://pmc.ncbi.nlm.nih.gov/articles/PMC4189812/
- *ACT for PTSD: Identifying Values* https://psychotherapyacademy.org/courses/act-for-trauma-witnessing-death/modules/from-avoidance-to-action-fostering-willingness-and-values/section/act-for-ptsd-identifying-values/
- *Discovering Your Natural Strengths After Trauma ...* https://blog.cyndibennettconsulting.com/unearthing-hidden-treasures-discovering-your-natural-strengths-after-trauma-554a658ed3e1
- *From Small Steps to Big Wins: The Importance of Celebrating* https://www.psychologytoday.com/us/blog/empower-your-mind/202406/from-small-steps-to-big-wins-the-importance-of-celebrating
- *Grounding Techniques | Article* https://www.therapistaid.com/therapy-article/grounding-techniques-article
- *The Polyvagal Theory and Healing Complex PTSD* https://drarielleschwartz.com/the-polyvagal-theory-and-healing-complex-ptsd-dr-arielle-schwartz/
- *The Container Method for Processing Trauma, PTSD and ...* https://therapyinanutshell.com/container-method/
- *Movement-Based Mindfulness: Bridging Somatic & ...* https://www.niroga.org/blogs/learn/mindful-movement-in-trauma-

recovery?srsltid=AfmBOorsAxkiNWHr7iPN6qqytmwGgfYlHFUL1KMYoF18BQfkG6dXp7Aj

- *Reparenting: Seeking Healing for Your Inner Child* https://positivepsychology.com/reparenting/
- *Inner Child Work: 15+ Practical Tools* https://positivepsychology.com/inner-child-healing/
- *Cultivating Self-Compassion in Trauma Survivors* https://self-compassion.org/wp-content/uploads/2015/08/Germer.Neff_.Trauma.pdf
- *80 Powerful Trauma Healing Affirmations* https://blog.innertune.com/healing-trauma-affirmations/
- *10 Tips to Set Healthy Boundaries after Trauma* https://northsidepsychology.com.au/10-tips-to-set-healthy-boundaries-after-trauma/
- *Module 6: How to Say "No" Assertively* https://www.cci.health.wa.gov.au/-/media/CCI/Consumer-Modules/Assert-Yourself/Assert-Yourself---06---How-to-Say-No-Assertively.pdf
- *6 Ways to Set Boundaries Without Guilt* https://www.psychologytoday.com/us/blog/conquering-codependency/202208/6-ways-set-boundaries-without-guilt
- *A Guide for Setting Boundaries in Relationships* https://www.lyrahealth.com/blog/boundaries-in-relationships/

- *Recognizing Safe People after Trauma* https://texaschristiancounseling.com/articles/recognizing-safe-people-after-trauma
- *The Power of Community in Trauma Survivorship* https://starmeadowcounseling.com/blog/the-power-of-community-in-trauma-survivorship/
- *Peer Support Groups - PTSD: National Center for PTSD - VA.gov* https://www.ptsd.va.gov/gethelp/peer_support.asp
- *Boundaries for Trauma Survivors* https://betterboundariesworkbook.com/boundaries-for-trauma-survivors/
- *Why Trauma Makes It Hard to Visualize a Positive Future* https://anniewright.com/trauma-and-difficulty-visualizing-the-future/
- *A Trauma Informed Approach to Setting Goals* https://www.myhealinghub.com/blog/a-trauma-informed-approach-to-setting-goals
- *The Power of Journaling: Structured Approaches for ...* https://cptsdfoundation.org/2023/08/02/the-power-of-journaling-structured-approaches-for-trauma-recovery/
- *Reclaiming joy after trauma* https://myndstories.com/reclaiming-joy-after-trauma-seema-girija-lal/
- *Addressing Religious or Spiritual Dimensions of Trauma and* ...

https://www.ptsd.va.gov/professional/treat/txessentials/spirituality_trauma.asp

- *Study: Trauma-Informed Bible Reading Reduces ...* https://www.christianitytoday.com/2021/05/bible-reading-study-trauma-ptsd-covid19-mental-health/
- *5 Steps to Build a Support Network for Trauma Recovery* https://www.ikonrecoverycenters.org/5-steps-to-build-a-support-network-for-trauma-recovery/
- *Growth after trauma* https://www.apa.org/monitor/2016/11/growth-trauma

Leave Review

www.ingramcontent.com/pod-product-compliance
Lightning Source LLC
LaVergne TN
LVHW022220200926
848481LV00006B/2050